Multilingual thesaurus on land tenure

English version

Edited by
Gérard Ciparisse

FOOD AND AGRICULTURE ORGANIZATION
OF THE UNITED NATIONS
Rome, 2003

This Thesaurus, published in the context of the World Food Summit: five years later, has been prepared with the financial support of Belgian Technical Cooperation.

ISBN 92-5-104283-7

Contents

Foreword

In November 1996, during the World Food Summit, the Heads of State and Government who met in Rome committed themselves to promoting equitable access by all to resources, be it land, water, forest or pasture, with a view to achieving food security and rural poverty alleviation.

This is why many delegations underlined, during the April 1997 session of FAO's Committee on Agriculture and in the spirit of World Food Summit follow-up, the need to take advantage of renewed interest shown by many countries in land tenure reform and in the different modes of accessing their natural resources.

In reply to these comments, the Rural Development Division proceeded to put in place an unambiguous and unequivocal terminology of the subjects related to land tenure in order to contribute to clarifying the debates in this field and to make related field interventions more efficient.

For this purpose, the Land Tenure Service (SDAA) of the Rural Development Division embarked on the preparation of a land tenure "Thesaurus", mainly covering the following sectors: legal, institutional, historical, description of space, traditional or written land tenure regulations, topographical, land management, as well as land tenure related information techniques.

It is expected that the Thesaurus will serve as reference material both for the normative divisions at FAO Headquarters as well as for field experts engaged in the implementation of projects with a land tenure component.

It could also be useful for training in subject matters related to natural resources and their management, as well as for researchers in the field of rural development.

It was planned that the original French version of the Land Tenure Thesaurus would be adapted to the specific socio-economic, institutional and historical contexts of the Spanish and English-speaking worlds, thus covering the three official working languages of the FAO and other UN agencies.

Adaptation of the French edition and not translation: in general, the words related to land tenure, if literally translated, do not reflect the full reality - whether perceived or experienced - of a different linguistic context.

Passing from one language to another also means passing from one socio-economic and agrarian context to another, the historic, institutional and legal evolution of which has given a certain connotation to the term, expression or concept used. We are therefore trying to transpose the various terms, as satisfactorily as possible, in the cultural as well as linguistic contexts in which they are used.

Synoptic reading of the various versions of the Thesaurus in the main working languages of FAO also allows for an understanding of the evolution of the different land tenure realities described in each language and illustrates the shades of meaning and different uses and comprehension of these realities in the working languages of the Organization.

This does not mean that we cannot further adapt the Thesaurus to other languages and institutional contexts, especially since land tenure is increasingly being considered as an essential aspect of rural development and agro-industrial production, in whatever language it is treated.

The agrarian structures are under constant transformation, although these changes might seem very slow at a first glance. Our effort to establish a terminology base should in fact be seen as an appeal to land tenure specialists, researchers and practitioners to enter into a dialogue with FAO's technical services in order to improve the contents of the Thesaurus by taking into account present land tenure problems.

Maximiliano Cox

Director
Rural Development Division

ACKNOWLEDGMENTS

The English version of the Thesaurus is the result of three series of interventions: first, collaboration between several FAO technical services that were invited to participate in the elaboration of the French version of the document on the various aspects of land tenure, which led to an initial list of terms most of which were divided into thematic chapters.

Based on this provisional terminology, Catherine Goislard, Juridical Anthropologist , proceeded to edit the first draft of the initial chapters.

Second, a team of researchers at the Catholic University of Leuven, linked to the Institute of Development Studies took over and completed the manuscript under the scientific coordination of Etienne Verhaegen, Agronomist, and the general supervision of Paul Mathieu, Socio-economist.

Nevertheless, it would not have been possible to produce the French version without the collaboration of land tenure specialists from various scientific research Institutes.

Third, the adaptation of the French version to the different land tenure English speaking countries' contexts, its review and the addition of terms were completed thanks to Mr. Paul Munro-Faure, former Director of the Commission 7 (Cadastre and Land Management) of the International Federation of Surveyors (FIG) who benefitted from the collaboration of Professor Peter Dale, University College, London, UK, Dr. Frances Plimmer, University of Glamorgan, UK, Professor Sue Nichols, University of New Brunswick, Canada, Markku Villikka, Executive Secretary, FIG and the Commissions, FIG, David Palmer, Land Tenure Service (FAO, SDAA), Fernando Fernández Arriaga (SDAA) and Alessandra Zorcolo, SDAA editorial Consultant.

Our thanks go to each and everyone who assisted in their own way, in the elaboration of this version of the Thesaurus.

Needless to say that any shortcomings or lacunae in the present version should be attributed solely to the editor, who asks readers to bring to his attention anything they would like to see included in a revised version of this modest Land Tenure Thesaurus.

Communications regarding the present adaptation should be addressed to the Chief, Land Tenure Service (SDAA), FAO, Viale delle Terme di Caracalla, 00100, Rome, Italy.

ILLUSTRATIONS

1. Parcels in the region of Quito, Ecuador.

2. A coastal zone in Sri Lanka, south of Colombo.

3. Zebra near the gates of Lake Mburo National park, midway between Masaka and Mbarara in western Uganda.

4. A Global Positioning System, an instrument to determine the precise location of locust's infestation. This information is transmitted to a centre in Tulear, Malagasy, which then organizes their elimination.

5. FAO expert discusses mapping and analysis of remote sensing data. Students are learning to use a mirror stereoscope (left) for aerial photos, and a stereopret (right), an instrument of topographical and contour-mapping use.

6. Land clearance in a hilly district of Japan.

7. Hydrology technician explaining the use of a motor pump to supply additional irrigation to farmers in Cambodia.

8. Agroforestry in practice in Zimbabwe. Food crops can be intercropped with trees.

Introduction

The English version of the *Multilingual Land Tenure Thesaurus* is an adaptation to the English-speaking countries of the French version published in 1999 [1].The publication includes key background information and references in addition to the basic definitions and provides examples where these help to clarify the sense and use of the term.

The English text follows the original French version's structure and includes a significant number of the equivalent terms that are used in common. Together with the Spanish version, these three versions cross-reference similar concepts and ideas to help readers understand the similarities and the differences between the three linguistic and legal traditions.

The entries are divided into chapters. Chapter I is general, and looks at the key players, the resources and the legal rights in land. Chapter II deals with issues of space, chapter III with policies, procedures and tools, chapter IV with information systems, chapter V with taxation and economics aspects, chapter VI with non-state regulation, and chapter VII with aspects of land that apply specifically to agricultural, pastoral and forestry activities.

The entries in each chapter are listed in alphabetical order. A general index at the end of the work brings together all of the principle entries in the thesaurus together with a number of secondary terms included in the entries.

Further development of this publication is planned to include additional initial versions in Chinese and Arabic. Following this, a process of assimilation and review will enable a substantially revised, Web-based, version to be developed for wider access and use.

1 Thesaurus multilingue du foncier. Version française. FAO. Rome: 1999.

I. PLAYERS, RESOURCES AND RIGHTS

CHAPTER 1

Players, resources and rights

1.A.1 Adverse possession

Adverse possession is the possession of land as a trespasser or squatter.

A trespasser or squatter can gain the right to possession after a statutorily prescribed period of limitation. The owner or person who has the right to possess the land can recover possession from a trespasser or squatter but the principle of limitation restricts this in time. In most countries the relevant period of limitation will be statutorily defined.

1.A.2 Alienation

Alienation is the transfer of ownership of land.

The owner of a freehold (fee simple absolute) under the English legal system has the right of alienation of the property during lifetime or by will after death. This means that the owner can transfer ownership of all or part of the property as he or she wishes, whether by sale or by gift.

In some traditional societies where there has been limited experience of land markets, the concept of alienation of land may not exist. Land may be conceived of as being held by those currently living in trust for their ancestors and those yet unborn. The act of permanent alienation is against this fundamental link between people and the land. In several such societies, pressures for alienation through the commoditisation of land have led to complications over who has the right to alienate the land. A common approach in the past to enable restricted dealings with such land, and yet to retain its essential inalienable nature has been through establishing appropriate customary practices or, in some cases, to create statutory trusts for land administration purposes. These trusts usually have rights to deal with such land in limited ways, thus trying to satisfy the traditional and the market economy oriented members of society.

1.A.3 Ancient lights / Right of light

A right of light, "ancient lights" consists of the right of the dominant tenement to sufficient light through defined apertures "according to the ordinary notions of mankind".
CARD, R., MURDOCH, J., SCHOFIELD, P., 1994

Ancient lights can only exist as an easement. The servient tenement cannot obstruct this right and thereby reduce the amount of light received. The rights to this easement may be created expressly or by implication, although most are acquired by prescription

The quantum of light required may vary according to the established use of the building in question. Industrial buildings, residential buildings and greenhouses have all been held to have different established requirements.

1.A.4 Assignment

An assignment is the transfer of a lease from the tenant to another party.

A tenant may be able to assign a lease to another party, although this right of assignment is likely to be constrained or prohibited by the terms of the lease agreement. By assigning the lease, the tenant transfers the entire remaining interest to another. This puts the new tenant, the assignee, in the same position vis-à-vis the landlord as the previous tenant.

A tenant has potentially very considerable rights of assignment and enjoyment associated with the leasehold interest that he or she enjoys, unless restricted by the terms of the lease. In circumstances where the tenant no longer wishes to hold the property there may be three choices available; assignment, sub-lease or surrender.

1.B.1 Beneficiary / Grantee

Attributaire (F); Asignatario / Adjudicatario (E)

A beneficiary is someone who derives advantage from something. A beneficiary under a will or a trust, for example, is someone who will have an interest under the will or trust.

1.C.1 Collective ownership

Propriété collective (F); Propiedad colectiva (E)

Collective ownership of a natural resource is where the holders of rights to a given natural resource are clearly defined as a collective group, and where they have the right to exclude third parties from the enjoyment of those rights. A collective farm such as the kolkhoz of the former Soviet Union involved a number of households working together in agricultural production.

1.C.2 Common property

Biens communaux (F); Bienes comunitarios (E)

Common property is typically land and other resources in which entitled beneficiaries, whether individual or community defined, have specific common rights. For example, community members can use a common pasture for grazing their cattle independently of one another. The community controls the use of the common property and can exclude non-members from using it.

Common property in this sense is distinct from "open access systems" where there is no control on access and no-one can be excluded.

1.C.3 Common rights

Common rights are rights held in common property.

1.C.4 Commons
Bien commun (F); Bien común (E)

The term "commons" is most frequently used to refer to those natural resources that are held in common by a community.

1.C.5 Communal ownership
Propiedad comunal (E)

"Communal ownership" is a commonly used term to describe those situations where rights to use resources are held by a community. It often includes communal rights to pastures and forests, and exclusive private rights to agricultural and residential parcels. In such community-based tenure regimes, people may not have the right to transfer their land to others, or may have strictly limited rights to transfer (e.g., transfers may be limited to heirs through inheritance, or sales may be restricted to members of the community.)

1.C.6 Concession
Concession (F); Concesión / Concesión inmobiliaria (E)

A concession is defined as the granting of a territory to a concessionaire for their occupation and use.

A "concession" is not a property right in English land law. There are, however, certain situations in some jurisdictions with an English law background where concessions are granted. It is common, for example, for oil and gas exploration and production licences in the UK and the US to be referred to as concessions, although both legally and in documentary terminology are licences.

Concessions are granted in ***Fiji*** *by the Native Land Trust Board for large scale indigenous forest exploitation. Since 1980 these long term concessions have included base annual rental payments, plus royalties based on the actual volume of timber extracted.*

1.C.7 Conservation easement

Conservation easements are partial interests in land designed to prevent development on conservation land.

Conservation easements have been developed principally in the US to protect land areas important for environmental reasons from development. They are typically long term, for example, 30 years, and are acquired in private land by government agencies and non-profit organisations for conservation purposes. They are typically negative, prohibiting certain actions, and are held "in gross", rather than "appurtenant" as the right is not held in respect of neighbouring property. They represent a market-oriented approach to conservation where a landowner gives up development rights over a specific area in return for a payment. WEIBE, K., TEGENE, A., KUHN, B., 1996

1.C.8 Contract

Contrat (F); Contrato (E)

A contract is a binding agreement on the parties to the contract.

For a contract to exist there must therefore be an agreement, and it must be intended by the parties that this agreement should be legally binding. The agreement must also be supported either by a deed or by consideration. Consideration is a promise or an act made by the promisee in return for the promisor's promise at the latter's express or implied request.

Most transactions in land comprise two stages. The first of these is a contractual stage where the parties formally agree the basis and terms of the bargain (contract). Up to the point of such agreement, negotiations will generally be flexible and offer and counter-offer made specifically "subject to contract". When the contract has been agreed, the second stage is the transfer or creation of the interest in land. Under some registration systems, transfer takes place on registration, and not on the execution of the contract.

1.C.9 Conveyance

The conveyance of land is the actual process of transfer of that land. A conveyance is a deed transferring land.

The legal definition of what is included in land is important as this governs what is conveyed. Fructus industriales (cultivated crops), for example, are typically excluded from a conveyance, but naturally growing things, fructus naturales, will be included. The procedures for conveyance vary according to the jurisdiction and according to the legal system for recording and transferring ownership.

Examples of the process of conveyance in a title registration regime include:
England and Wales: *The process of conveyance depends on whether the land being conveyed is registered or not.*

Where the land being conveyed is registered, the register of title maintained by HM Land Registry will be relied on, together with any further particulars arising from questions relating to the title. An official search of the register will generate an official certificate of search. This certificate provides a definitive statement of title and confers a priority period of 30 days from the date of application. The transaction should be completed and the purchaser should apply to be registered as proprietor during this period. It is this registration as proprietor in the Land Registry that vests in the purchaser the legal estate. The purchaser is indemnified against any error in the official search.

Where unregistered land is being conveyed the process is complicated by the need for the demonstration of a good root of title. This requires a clear tracing of all of the dealings in the land until the time of transaction for a period of at least 15 years. In this case, the completion takes place when the conveyance deed is completed and the purchase consideration paid, when the legal title passes to the purchaser. All sales of freeholds are now compulsorily registered, and the purchaser must apply for first registration to HM Land Registry within two months of completion, otherwise the legal estate reverts to the vendor.

1.C.10 Co-ownership / Undivided shares

Copropriétaire (F); Copropietario / Comunero (E)

Co-ownership is where two or more people have ownership together of a freehold or leasehold interest. The enjoyment of a property in co-ownership is said to be in undivided shares, in that each person has the same right to any part of the property.

There are two forms of co-ownership; joint tenancy and tenancy in common.

A joint tenancy exists where there is:

> right of survivorship (on the death of a joint tenant their right passes to the remaining joint tenants, until only one remains as the sole owner)
> unity of possession (no joint owner can exclude another)
> unity of interest (each joint tenant is jointly entitled to the entire interest in the property)
> unity of title (all joint tenants in a property derive their title under the same document)
> unity of time (all joint tenants' interests must commence at the same time.

With a tenancy-in-common, by contrast, there is no right of survivorship as each tenant-in-common has a fixed, although undivided, share that at death can, for example, be passed on by will to any designated successor. Unity of possession is a characteristic requirement of tenancy-in common and although usually present, the other unities are not essential.

1.C.11 Custom / Use / User

Coutumes / Coutumier (F);
Costumbres / Consuetudinario (E)

Custom results from practice since time immemorial.

Use rights can be created in land on the basis of custom. These rights are often created by the use of the land over a long period of time.

They are often the rights created by ancestral occupation and use of land by traditional societies. The creation and recognition of boundaries where these exist for such land will often use natural features, or planted trees or hedges.

Although custom and customary use rights are most frequently associated with traditional societies, western societies may also recognise such rights.

Examples of customary use right in a traditional society include:
Samoa: *Customary land title is enshrined in the constitution and its alienation is prohibited, although leasing and taking for public purposes is allowed. Almost 80% of all land in Samoa is under customary tenure. Most of this is not surveyed or registered and is still held by the extended family group (aiga) under the control of the chief (pule). THOMAS, P., 1984*

Examples of the recognition of a customary use right in a western society include:
England and Wales: *General customs were typically absorbed into either judicial precedent (Common Law) or statute starting particularly in the seventeenth and eighteenth centuries. Local customs, however, still exist and are occasionally recognised by the courts as a variance of the general law. Such customs are now of very limited significance and generally relate to rights of way or of common. To demonstrate the existence of a customary right, it must be shown to:*

- *have existed since time immemorial (taken as being since 1189, although generally presumed providing the oldest living inhabitant can affirm the right and that it could have been in existence in 1189)*
- *have been continuous*
- *not be unreasonable*
- *be certain*
- *be recognised as compulsory*
- *not be contradicted by statute or a fundamental principal of the common law*

1.D.1 Deed

A deed is a written or printed instrument that effects a legal disposition such as a contract for sale.

Traditionally under English law a deed was a document that was "signed, sealed and delivered". Since 1989 these requirements have been relaxed, with the removal of the requirement to seal a deed. It must be clear that the document is intended to be a deed. For the deed to be executed it now requires simply to be signed the individual party to the deed in the presence of two witnesses who attest the signature. The process of delivery now no longer has to be a physical delivery, it is enough that there are acts to show that the maker of the deed intends to be unconditionally bound by it.

1.D.2 Dominant tenement

A dominant tenement is a property that enjoys the benefit of a right of easement. An easement often requires that there should be a dominant tenement that enjoys the right of easement, such as a right of way, over a servient tenement.

1.D.3 Dowry

Dot (F); Dote (E)

A dowry is the property that forms a part of a marriage agreement. The dowry is traditionally the property provided to the marriage by the family of the bride. The practice remains an important part of some cultures, particularly those that are based in the East.

1.E.1 Easement

Easements are rights exercisable by owners of one parcel of land over other land.

Easements fall into two groups, positive and negative. Thus easements include those where someone has a positive right to do something over another person's land, such as exercising a right of way, and those where an owner has a right to stop someone doing something on their land, such as a right to light (ancient lights).

The creation of an easement often requires that there should be a dominant and a servient tenement. There should in other words be land that benefits from the easement, and land that provides the easement; the owners of the two tenements should be different. It is also important that the easement is capable of being the subject of a grant.

In some cases, such as with a conservation easement, there is a servient tenement but no dominant tenement as there is no requirement for the holder of the easement rights to own other land.

1.E.2 Encumbrance / Servitude
Servitude (F); Servidumbre (E)

An encumbrance on the land is a right adversely affecting the land.

Encumbrances include a number of burdens. Many are registrable in formal real estate registration systems; such as restrictive covenants, easements, mortgages and registered leases. An encumbrance is broadly similar to a servitude, a term commonly used in continental European jurisdictions but infrequently used in English law.

Some such rights are not registrable under English law, and these overriding interests must be checked for by enquiry and inspection. They include legal easements, "squatters' rights acquired or being acquired under the Limitation Acts, rights of those in actual occupation or receiving the rents or profits from the land, and leases for terms of not more than 21years.

1.E.3 Entail

An entail in English law restricts succession to land to direct lineal descent and is intended to keep land in the same family.

A freehold property can be entailed by creating a fee tail. This form of inheritable ownership restricts succession to the land in question to direct lineal descendants of the original grantor. It effectively creates a succession of life interests. These interests were legal estates prior to the Law of Property Act, 1925, but since then are regarded as equitable interests. They are now relatively infrequently encountered.

1.E.4 Equitable interest

Equitable interests are interests in English law that derive from the law of equity.

English law is based on a set of canons of law; statute, Common Law and equity. Equitable interests in land include those interests that are not defined as legal estates in land, including those broadly speaking of a commercial nature, such as restrictive covenants and mortgages, and those of a family nature, such as life interests or interests in co-ownership. The Law of Property Act, 1925, defined only two statutory legal estates in land, the freehold and the leasehold. All other interests in land, such as those identified, therefore are, or became as a result, equitable interests.

1.E.5 Estoppel

Estoppel is the prevention of a course of action by a person or entity by their own prior action.

An interest in land can be created in equity where a landowner creates or encourages an expectation on the part of someone that he or she will have an interest in the land. Where that person takes possession of the land and subsequently invests money in the anticipation of that expectation, then, the courts in equity will give effect to the expectation. This creation of an interest in land in equity is known as proprietary estoppel.

1.E.6 Eviction

Déguerpissement (F); Desalojo / Despojo / Lanzamiento (E)

Eviction is the removal of someone from their occupation of land or property.

The term is very commonly used in connection with the eviction of squatters, but may also be used in the context of unlawful eviction and harassment. In the latter case, landlords have been held liable for attempting to drive out tenants in lawful occupation of a property. This has usually involved the landlord breaching the covenant, actual or implied by a tenancy, that the tenant should benefit from the quiet enjoyment of the property. The remedy of the tenant has generally been in damages, although statutory entitlements to damages may also be specified.

1.F.1 Fee simple absolute

The fee simple absolute, also known as the freehold, is full ownership of land in English law, providing the owner with the largest 'bundle of rights' of ownership.

1.F.2 Fishing rights / Piscary

Fishing rights are specified rights to fish, whether in freshwater or in marine areas. The nature of fishing rights varies according to the jurisdiction but distinctions are often made between rights for marine fishing and those for freshwater or inland fishing.

In the UK it is usual for fishing rights to be considered differently whether they are marine fishing rights or freshwater fishing rights. In the United Kingdom most offshore commercial marine fishing rights are controlled through the EU's Common Fisheries Policy. Some commercial marine fishing rights, such as netting for salmon, are controlled by the relevant government department, while others, such as fixed or estuarine coastal nets for salmon, are frequently privately owned. Fishing for marine shellfish is often free access. Freshwater fishing rights are usually an integral part of the landowner's riparian rights that extend out to the middle stream of a river. They may also, however, have been separated from the landownership and be owned as a separate legal interest, or may exist as a distinct customary right.

Examples of reassertion of indigenous peoples' rights in fisheries in marine areas include:
New Zealand: *The government of New Zealand's proposals to issue fishing quotas under the Fisheries Amendment Act, 1986 resulted in claims that this would result in sales of fishing rights that Maori people had not relinquished. It was argued that this was contrary to the principles of the Waitangi Treaty, which envisaged the protection of Maori fishing interests. The claim was subsequently heard by the Waitangi Tribunal and the decision given that the Maori people could demonstrate their rights in relation to fisheries at the time of the Treaty and that they should therefore be entitled to the revenue from the quota. WAITANGI TRIBUNAL, 1988*

Examples of assertion of indigenous peoples' rights in fisheries in freshwater areas include:
Canada: *Representatives of the indigenous peoples of Canada, the First Nation peoples, signed treaties in the late 1800s and early 1900s with the government of Canada to protect the right of Status Indians to fish for food at any time of the year. In Manitoba, fish stock conservation to ensure resource sustainability, is the first priority for making management decisions. Following this, domestic fishing for food by First Nations peoples is given the highest priority for harvest of the fishery resource. These rights are protected under Canada's Constitution.*

1.F.3 Freehold

Freehold, the everyday equivalent of the technical legal term fee simple absolute, is full ownership of land in English law, providing the owner with the largest 'bundle of rights' of ownership.

1.F.4 Fructus industriales

Fructus industriales are cultivated crops. Generally speaking in English land law, fructus industriales will not be regarded as a part of the land in a conveyance, and will form a part of a tenant's claim for tenant right compensation at the end of a tenancy.

1.F.5 Fructus naturales

Fructus naturales are things that grow naturally on the land which do not require annual attention, such as apple trees.
Generally speaking in English land law, fructus naturales will be regarded as a part of the land in a conveyance.

1.H.1 Hereditament

A hereditament is real property that can be inherited, such as, for example, a freehold or a leasehold.

1.H.2 Hierarchy of courts

The hierarchy of courts is the structure of the legal administrative system of a given jurisdiction.

Examples of hierarchies of courts include:

England and Wales: *The lowest levels of courts are the magistrates courts and the county courts. The latter is particularly involved with land related issues with jurisdiction over actions in contract and tort, for the recovery of land and for certain types of equity including, for example, in administration of estates or in foreclosures on mortgages. A ceiling is set for the value of the action above which it is usually considered by the High Court. Appeals from the High Court are generally heard by the Court of Appeal.*

The High Court, the Crown Court and the Court of Appeal comprise the Supreme Court of Judicature, with the Crown Court having principally a criminal jurisdiction. The various divisions of the High Court deal with various jurisdictions including those where real estate is an important element. Appeal from both of these courts is generally to the Court of Appeal.

The Appellate Committee of the House of Lords hears appeals from the Court of Appeal and in some cases direct from the High Court. The highest court of appeal since the UK joined the EU is the European Court.

Several specialist functions are fulfilled by specific tribunals. The Lands Tribunal, for example, deals with appeals from local valuation tribunals on rating issues, assessments of compensation where agreement cannot be reached, and other property related issues Appeals from the Lands Tribunal on a point of law are generally heard by the Court of Appeal.

The Judicial Committee of the Privy Council continues to fulfil an appellate function for a limited number of Commonwealth countries, including for example New Zealand and Jamaica.

1.L.1 Land
Fonds (F); Fundo / Heredad / Finca (E)

Land in a legal sense is real estate.

1.L.2 Land law
Droit foncier (F); Derecho de tierras (E)

Land law is the body of law dealing with land, its definition, ownership and use whether urban or rural.

1.L.3 Land ownership

Land ownership in the English Common Law context is comprised of a set of rights in land held by the owner.

Technically in England and Wales land is held from the Crown as the ultimate owner. Land ownership rights include in this context the natural rights of support, of a free flow of air and of water where appropriate. They also include the right to alienate or dispose of the whole or part of the interest to whomsoever, and on whatever terms as to sale, rent or gift the owner and acquirer please. The rights of enjoyment enjoyed by the owner of the freehold are the widest possible, consistent with not interfering with the rights of others or with statutory restrictions. The freeholder has the right to enjoy all that is on, beneath or above the land and has the right to use and even to waste the land if he or she wishes.

1.L.4 Land tenure system

Faire-valoir / modes de faire-valoir (F); Formas de explotación / modos de aprovechamiento (E)

The land tenure system in a given jurisdiction comprises the set of possible bases under which land may be used. As such this range encompasses both rural and urban tenures and includes ownership, tenancy and other arrangements for the use of land.

The land tenure system in an English Common Law based jurisdiction will, to a greater or lesser extent, usually comprise a range of different types of tenures.

Examples of a land tenure system where the tenure structure accommodates both English land law based tenure and indigenous land tenure include:
Fiji: *Around 88% of Fiji's land is held under customary tenure by the indigenous Fijian people. Ownership is determined according to a hierarchy of family relationships which are recorded by the Native Land and Fisheries Commissioners. Native land is inalienable and is categorised according to whether or not the land is in native reserve. Land is leased through the Native Land Trust Board which administers land under a statutory trust. Leasing of native reserve land is restricted principally to indigenous Fijians. Native land which is not leased is used by the owners following customary practices.*

The balance of land is either state land or freehold land. State land is administered by the government according to statute, and is usually leased to tenants.

All of these tenures are affected by overriding legislation affecting landlord and tenant relations. In particular, the agricultural sector has been greatly affected by the Agricultural Landlord and Tenant Act.

Examples of a land tenure system that has developed in the Common Law and has been largely formalised into statute include:
England and Wales: *The land tenure system is based on the freehold and leasehold system, although other informal and, less importantly, customary arrangements also provide flexible access to land. The keystones of this much simplified system date largely from 1925 and the passing of several pivotal pieces of legislation. These tenures were originally developed in the Common Law but are now enshrined in statute.*

1.L.5 Landlord
Propriétaire (F); Dueño / Dueña (E)

A landlord is a person or entity receiving rent from a tenant.

When an owner of land leases that land to another, the tenant is known as the lessee and the owner as the lessor or landlord. The term landlord is widely used to refer to any person leasing or subleasing land and may thus also refer to a tenant who is subleasing land to a subtenant.

1.L.6 Lease
Bail (F); Arrendamiento / Arriendo (E)

A lease is a contractual agreement between a landlord and a tenant for the tenancy of land.

A lease or tenancy agreement is the contractual document used to create a leasehold interest or tenancy. The period of the lease is known as the "term" of the lease. A lease requires the following as a part of the agreement. The lease should be for a definite period, or for a period that is capable of definition. The date of commencement should be fixed, and the date of termination either fixed, or capable of being fixed. The lease should provide to the tenant the right to exclusive possession of the land, thus giving the lessee the right to exclude others, including the landlord, from the land. Where exclusive possession is not granted, the occupation will generally be regarded as a licence.

The lease will generally include a set of undertakings or covenants by the landlord and the tenant. These usually include tenant's covenants to pay rent and taxes, to keep the premises in repair, to allow the lessor to view the state of repair of the property and, on the lessor's part to allow the tenant the quiet enjoyment of the property. In addition, a condition of reentry will usually be inserted in the event of the tenant's non-payment of rent (forfeiture). There are in addition certain implied rights and obligations on the part of the lessee and lessor, including for example the right of the lessee to reap crops that have been sown (emblements). Express covenants in addition to the usual covenants that are likely to be included are those not to assign or sublet, and to insure against fire ad other specified risks.

1.L.7 **Legal**
Légal (F); Legal (E)

The term "legal" describes an action or thing that conforms with the law.

1.L.8 **Legislation**
Législation (F); Legislación (E)

Legislation is the body of laws which make up the law and comprises the formal laws passed by the legislature together with any subordinate legislation, including regulations and statutory instruments.

1.L.9 **Lessee / Tenant**
Locataire (F); Arrendatario / Inquilino (E)

A lessee holds a lease or tenancy of land under a lease contract or tenancy entered into with a lessor or landlord.

1.L.10 Licence

Permis d'occuper (F)

A licence confers on the licensee a right to enter land but does not grant a legal interest in that land.

A licence covers a wide range of agreements. An example is a timber licence which grants a person the right to enter land to harvest timber.

1.L.11 Life interest

A life interest is an interest enjoyed for a life.

In English law a life interest is usually created by a settlement entailing the land or by a specific grant. Since 1925 in England and Wales, a life interest is an equitable interest. The tenant for life will generally be liable for waste, unless this is specifically excluded in the grant. The life tenant may sell the interest in which case it continues to be enjoyed for the life of the original life tenant and is said to be held *pur autre vie*.

1.L.12 Local community

Collectivité territoriale ou locale (F);
Colectividad territorial o local (E)

Local community has no standard definition. It will typically be defined according to the circumstances. These may be relatively informal where the management of common property resources is concerned. They may be formal, and statutorily based where dealing with planning issues.

Local communities are involved to varying degrees in decisions and activities relating to the use of land within their jurisdictions. The actual level of local community responsible for a given decision or activity will depend on how the local administration is structured and what powers are allocated to the respective tiers of the administration.

1.M.1 Management rights

Droit de gestion (F); Derecho de gestión (E)

Management rights are the rights of the owner to manage the interest in land in accordance with the limitations imposed by the interest.

The possession of land, whether under the legal estates of fee simple or leasehold, or in various interests in equity, such as a life interest, confers specific rights in relation to the management of that legal estate or interest. The rights associated with some estates and interests are wider than others. For example, the fee simple absolute has the greatest possible rights being perpetual, providing the widest scope for management. Leasehold interest rights are more limited, both in duration and the nature of the rights, as the lessee is liable for waste during the term of the lease.

1.O.1 Occupation / Possession / Squatting

Occupation (Envahissement / Appropriation) (F);
Ocupación / Invasión / Usucapión (E)

Occupation is the physical occupation of land.

Occupation is distinct in English law from possession. The latter may involve occupation, or it may simply be the right to receive rents or profits from the land in question. It is generally a matter of fact, although legally speaking the fact of occupation may, for example, be established by an employee or representative of the claimant.

The occupation of land may be significant in creating a number of interests in land. In particular it may create overriding interests that are not registered under the system of land registration. In order to identify any occupier's rights it is necessary to inspect the land and to make enquiries of the vendor about the situation.

1.O.2 Occupier

Occupant (F)

The occupier of land is the person who is in occupation of that land.

1.O.3 Owner / Proprietor

Propriétaire (F); Propietario (E)

The owner of land is the person who owns the relevant legal interest in the land as recognised by the law.

The owner does not necessarily possess the land, as for example, when it is leased or adversely possessed by another.

1.O.4 Owner-occupier

The owner-occupier of land is one who both owns and occupies the land.

1.P.1 Parcel

Parcelle (F); Parcela (E)

A parcel (or plot) of land is an area of land with a particular ownership, land use, or other characteristic.

A parcel is frequently used as the basis for a cadastre or land registration system.

"The basic spatial unit in a cadastre is known as a parcel. A parcel can be defined in many ways depending on the purpose of the cadastre. For instance, an area with a particular type of land use may be considered a parcel in some systems; in others it is defined as an area exclusively controlled or owned by an individual or group of individuals (e.g. family or corporation). In some systems a property may consist of several parcels of land which may be distributed over a small region such as a village. The flexibility in the definition makes it possible to adapt the cadastral system to particular needs and thus also to adapt the cost of the registration. If, for instance, the purpose is mainly to protect the ongoing traditional land use, larger parcels representing common interests can be defined as the basis for the system." FIG, 1995

IMAGE 1

1.P.1 Parcel

Parcels in the region of Quito, Ecuador.

Photo: Yann-Arthus Bertrand.
La Terre vue du Ciel. Editions de La Martinière.

1.P.2 Party wall

Party walls are structures that may be used to define boundaries under a 'general boundaries' principle.

Under English law the definition of boundaries is usually under the "general boundaries" principle. Boundaries in such circumstances are not specifically surveyed but are marked on Ordnance Survey maps for conveyancing and registration purposes. In many cases some form of boundary structure is erected to mark the boundary. Some boundary structures are clearly on one side of the boundary and within that side's ownership. Others are over the boundary line and mark it directly. Where this is the case, the law usually divides the ownership vertically with each side having a right of support from the other. Such boundary structures, whether they are walls, hedges or ditches are known in legal terms as "party walls".

1.P.3 Periodic tenancy

A periodic tenancy is a monthly or weekly tenancy that continues indefinitely until proper notice of the relevant period is given.

1.P.4 Personal property / Moveable property / Chattel

Meuble / Mobilier (F); Mueble mobiliario (E)

A chattel, also known as a fixture, is a movable, personal property, such as cattle. It is distinct from the real property interest.

1.P.5 Planning permission

Planning permission is the grant of permission for a specified development under the relevant legislation.

Planning permission in the United Kingdom dates from the 1947 Town and Country Planning Act. Although this legislation has subsequently been revised and consolidated, it remains essentially the same, with planning permission required for anything that constitutes "development". This is defined as almost anything requiring building, engineering, mining or other operations, or material changes of use. The requirement for planning permission generally has extended down to the low water mark. Although agriculture and forestry were originally largely exempted from planning constraints, recent legislation has considerably reduced these exemptions.

Where planning permission is refused, appeals may be made to the relevant government ministry and will be heard by a planning inspector appointed for the purpose. Further appeal is available to the Court of Appeal on a point of law. Planning permission is distinct from building regulations approval which is administered under the Public Health Acts.

1.P.6 Possession
Possession (F); Posesión (E)

Possession of land may involve physical occupation with or without permission from the owner, or the right to receive rents or profits from the land.

1.P.7 Prescription
Prescription (F); Prescripción (E)

Prescription is the acquisition or extinction of rights by lapse of time.

Prescription is the way in which property rights may be legally acquired through possession for a period of time that is continued, peaceable, and without lawful interruption for the legally stipulated period. Under English Law, prescription is restricted to incorporeal rights such as easements. Under Roman law, prescription applies to ownership over parcels of land as well.

1.P.8 Private property
Propriété privée (F); Propiedad privada (E)

Private property is property that is held privately, whether individually, jointly or corporately. Private property and the associated rights of ownership are a keystone of market economies. In those countries that have written constitutions, the right to hold private property is usually enshrined as a fundamental human right.

Although different economic systems have different attitudes to the private ownership of real property, the human right to hold private property is generally acknowledged. The Universal Declaration of Human Rights of the UN includes at Article 17 that (1) Everyone has the right to own property alone as well as in association with others. (2) No one shall be arbitrarily deprived of his property.

1.P.9 Property law (real / immovable)

Droit immobilier (F); Derecho inmobiliario (E)

Property law is the generic term within which falls all of the legal framework dealing with property, its use, ownership, regulation and disposition. As such, property law applies both to real property and personal property, and is distinguished from land law, which applies only to real property.

1.P.10 Protected tenancy

A protected tenancy is one that enjoys the protection of statute under the relevant landlord and tenant legislation.

1.R.1 Real property / Immoveable / Real estate

Propriété immobilière (F); Raíz / Inmueble / Bienes raíces / Bienes inmuebles (E)

Real property or real estate is a generic term for land and buildings.

The terms, real property and real estate, arise from the concept of a "real" action which allowed an owner who was wrongly deprived of land to recover it. In contrast, in the case of moveable or personal property, a "personal" action allowed for compensation for wrongful dispossession and not for the return of the object.

1.R.2 Reform
Réforme (F); Reforma (E)

A reform is a modification of an existing law or institution, either by the revision of an existing law or by the enactment of a new law.

Reforms are the expression of changing technical, economic, social and political perspectives and preferences through the legislature. The process of reform in a parliamentary democracy on the lines of the Westminster parliament involves a series of stages whereby a proposal for a law moves towards effective enactment.

1.R.3 Regime
Régime (F); Régimen (E)

A regime is the general system of government of a country or an organisation, comprising the laws and administrative institutions viewed as a whole.

1.R.4 Rent
Redevance / Loyer (F); Canon / Renta / Renta fija (E)

The rent is the periodic sum, often weekly, monthly, quarterly or annually, paid under a lease or tenancy agreement in return for the use of the property.

Rentals may be fixed according to the prevailing market values, which tends to encourage more efficient use of the property because the more efficient tenants will be able to afford the higher rents. It is common practice for there to be regular revision of rents. Although the arrangements vary from market to market, two common approaches are for regular reviews to the current full rental value based on comparable rentals recently agreed, or for rents to be reviewed on the basis of changes in the retail prices index.

It is often the case for rents to be fixed administratively where publicly owned land is leased, or for rents to be controlled below market rental values as the result of protective landlord and tenant legislation.

Rents that are currently at the full market rental value (broadly the rental that would reasonably be expected to be agreed between a willing lessor and a lessee) are referred to as rack rents, and such properties are rack rented.

Where the existing rent, or rent passing, is less than the full rental value, a profit rent is said to exist, and this creates value in the leasehold interest, varying according to its duration.

In some cases the landlord may demand or decide to accept a capital sum from the tenant in lieu of rent at the outset of the lease. This is known as a premium, and the rent will often be referred to as a ground rent. Where the rent is negligible it is commonly referred to as a peppercorn rent.

1.R.5 Restrictive covenant

A restrictive covenant as defined in English land law is a restriction in favour of the dominant land which imposes a burden on the servient land.

A restrictive covenant has to be negative in substance, restricting the servient land in some way, very commonly as regards its use. Restrictive covenants may range from restrictions on types and sizes of buildings to prohibiting the hanging of clothes washing outside.

1.R.6 Reversion

The reversion of a property is enjoyed by the freeholder, as original grantor, on the death of a life tenant. The term is also used to describe the landlord's interest in the land for the period after the term of a lease has expired. This is the point at which the freeholder is entitled to regain occupation at Common Law. In practice statute law, through relevant landlord and tenant legislation, has modified this right considerably, thus restricting the ability of the freeholder or landlord to remove a tenant.

1.R.7 Right of enjoyment / Usufruct
Droit de jouissance / Droit d'usufruit (F);
Derecho de usufructo o goce (E)

The rights of enjoyment of the owner of the fee simple are very wide and include the right to do whatever he or she wishes on the land providing it doesn't interfere with the legal rights of others. The owner is further restricted in the unfettered enjoyment of the land by statute, most significantly as to use by the Town and Country Planning Acts, as to building by the Public Health Acts, and as to landlord and tenant relations by a string of relevant laws.

A life tenant has more restricted rights of enjoyment of the land and would generally, for example, be liable for waste unless specifically excluded in the grant.

1.R.8 Right of pre-emption
Droit de préemption (F);
Derecho de preferencia / Prelación (E)

A right of pre-emption is the right of first refusal enjoyed by the holder of the right which requires the vendor of the land to give the holder the first opportunity to buy on agreed terms.

In effect, the right of pre-emption becomes an option as soon as the owner takes steps showing a desire to sell.

Statutory rights of pre-emption are not a typical feature of land management regimes based on English Common Law. In France, and French law influenced regimes, the right of pre-emption in favour of neighbouring farmers is a common provision. These are administered in France, for example, by the rural SAFER organisations.

1.R.9 Right of way

Rights of way may be either private or public. A private right of way is an easement, conferring the right of way only on the owner of the dominant tenement over the servient tenement. A public right of way is a right of "highway" enjoyed by the general public.

1.R.10 Rights

Droit (F); Derechos (E)

Rights are defined by the legal framework and provisions under a given regime.

Different societies have different attitudes and so the nature of these rights varies, notwithstanding that there are some rights that are fairly universally acknowledged under declarations such as the Universal Declaration of Human Rights.

The owner of real estate enjoys a wide range of rights including, where appropriate; natural rights (support, air), rights of alienation, rights of enjoyment (freedom of use, everything in, on or above the land, waste). Where property rights are infringed it is common for there to be some form of compensation.

1.R.11 Riparian rights

Riparian rights are those rights in respect of the use and entitlement to water enjoyed by a riparian owner whose land is contiguous with a river or stream.

A riparian owner under English land law has the right to a flow of river or stream of substantially unaltered quality and quantity. A riparian owner may take adequate water for domestic purposes and the watering of cattle. If water is taken for any other purposes, a similar quantity and quality of water must be returned to the watercourse. The riparian owner also enjoys the rights to fish in non-tidal waters. Where opposite banks are in different ownership these rights extend to the middle of the stream.

1.S.1 Servient tenement

A servient tenement is a property that is subject to a right of easement.

An easement requires that there should be a servient tenement that is subject to a right of easement, such as a right of way, enjoyed by a dominant tenement

1.S.2 Squatter

A squatter is a person who takes unauthorised possession of unoccupied premises. Under English law, a squatter may acquire title to the property by adverse possession and the operation of Limitation Acts.

1.S.3 State property

Propriété de l'Etat / étatique (F);
Propiedad fiscal / Propiedad pública (E)

State property is property owned by the State. Different regimes adopt different approaches to the identification of state property.

The feudal system from which English land law stems identifies the Crown (the personification of the State) as the source of all land ownership, as the ultimate owner of all land. In another sense the State is an owner of land as property in the same way as any other owner, public or private, and will acquire or dispose of land and enjoy the same rights as any other land owner. In a third sense the State's over-riding capacity to control land through, for example, town and country planning, reflects the fact that the rights of the land owner may be limited by the State.

1.S.4 Statute law

Droit écrit (F); Derecho escrito (E)

Statute law is that part of the legal system that is delivered by parliament, and is distinct in English Common Law countries from judicial precedent in which law is developed by the decisions of the Courts.

1.S.5 Subtenant

Subarrendatario (E)

A subtenant is the lessee of a tenant where the tenant chooses (usually with the required permission of the landlord) to create a smaller leasehold interest.

A subtenant's interest must be for a period less than that enjoyed by the tenant, and is often for the remaining term less a few days. The tenant in such an arrangement retains the rights and responsibilities of a tenant to the landlord rather than assigning the whole remaining tenancy to another and passing on those rights and responsibilities as far as the law allows. It is therefore possible for a chain of tenancies to develop out of the original freehold.

1.T.1 Tenancy

A tenancy is a lease or a periodic tenancy.

1.T.2 Tenant / Tenant farmer / Lessee

Tenancier (F); Tenedor (E)

A tenant is a lessee who has the exclusive right of possession of premises under a lease. The lease is granted by the landlord or lessor.

1.T.3 Tenant right

Tenant right, in an agricultural context, is a specific group of rights of a tenant to compensation from the landlord at the end of a tenancy.

Examples of tenant right include:
England and Wales: *The agricultural tenant under the Agricultural Holdings Act, 1986, has specific statutory entitlements in respect of disturbance and improvements. The tenant has in addition compensation payable in respect of tenant right. These include:*

> *for any growing crops or harvested crops and products having been grown or produced on the holding during the last year of the tenancy (excluding those which the tenant is allowed to sell or remove from the holding)*

> *seed sown, cultivations, fallows, and other acts of husbandry at the expense of the tenant pasture laid down at the expense of the tenant, unless agreed as an obligation with the landlord, or paid for by the tenant on taking entry of the holding*

> *hefting (acclimatisation) of hill sheep on hill land in certain circumstances any residual manurial/ fertility value of the soil.*

1.T.4 Tenure
Tenure (F); Tenencia (E)

Tenure is the relationship, whether legally or customarily defined, among people as individuals or groups, with respect to land and associated natural resources. Rules of tenure define how property rights in land are to be allocated within societies. Land tenure systems determine who can use what resources for how long, and under what conditions.

1.T.5 Timeshare
Jouissance à temps partagé (F);
Posesión compartida por tiempos limitados (E)

A timeshare is a means of dividing a property on the basis of time, most commonly on a weekly basis.

A timeshare is a means of dividing a property to make it more marketable and to realise greater proceeds from the sale than if sold as a whole. In principle it is a form of multiple ownership. It is for example quite possible to have a leasehold timeshare, in which case the lease is of the specified period, usually by the week, over the term of the lease. This approach is particularly commonly used in the sale of holiday properties.

1.T.6 Title
Titre foncier (F); Título de tierras / Escritura pública / Título de propiedad (E)

The title to a property is the basis of its ownership.

In the context of English land law this is a function of the doctrine of estates and the doctrine of tenure. In order to prove title under the pre-registration title deeds system or in unregistered land in England and Wales, it was necessary to be able to demonstrate a clear root of title going back at least 15 years. With registered land, the fact of registration acts as proof of title in the quality registered. Appropriate searches and enquiries still have to be made, however, to ensure that there are no over-riding interests that may affect the title.

1.T.7 Transaction costs

Coûts de transaction (F); Costos de transacción / Compromiso o promesa de compraventa (E)

Transaction costs are the costs associated with the transaction of property. Transaction costs include both time and money. Time involved in some of the processes may be considerable, particularly for example where registration is undertaken personally. The money costs will generally include some or all of the following:

- agent's fees for the sale of the property (usually expressed as a percentage of the transaction sum)
- lawyer'sfees
- stamp or transaction duty or tax
- value added tax
- registration fees

1.T.8 Trespasser

A trespasser is generally defined as someone who goes onto land without any invitation of any sort and whose presence is either unknown to the proprietor or, if known, is practically objected to. The distinction between a trespasser and a lawful visitor may be important in identifying liability in the event of misadventure.

1.U.1 Unclaimed land

Terres vacantes (F); Tierras vacantes / Baldíos (E)

Unclaimed land is land for which there is no owner or claimant.
The concept of unclaimed land does not practically arise in England and Wales because all land is owned, as there will always be someone with the superior title, if only the Crown. The idea has, however, been of particular significance during the process of colonisation by the European powers. A common approach in such circumstances in Africa, for example, was for the colonising power to enact legislation extinguishing customary claims over land deemed unoccupied and to then issue leasehold or freehold titles to new occupants, generally colonist settlers. BRUCE, J. W., and MIGOT-ADHOLLA, S., 1994

In the former French colonial territotories, where the concept of *terres vacantes et sans maître* remains often a part of the legal framework, it is now considered that there remains effectively no basis for such a claim as all land, whether fallow, reserve or bush will usually be under some person or group.

> *Examples of the use of the concept of unclaimed or vacant land include:*
> ***Australia:*** *The original settlement of Australia in the late 18th Century was based on the concept of terra nullius, in that there did not appear to the first settlers to be any established system of law on the continent. A system of law based on English practice was therefore established and freehold grants and leasehold interests were created. In 1992 the High Court established in the Mabo Judgement that native title had in fact existed in 1788 and that it has survived in those areas where it has not been extinguished by freehold.*

1.U.2 Use right
Droit d'usage / Usus (F); Uso / Usuario (E)

The use right or right to use land is one of the essential rights of land ownership.

In some continental European jurisdictions the usufruct is the right to use and take the profits from immovable property as though the owner, but with a duty of preservation. The usufruct may endure for life, or it may be for a specified number of years. In the latter case it is terminated on the death of the beneficiary. In some jurisdictions the right may be transferable. The nearest equivalent in English law is the life interest where the life tenant will be liable for waste.

1.V.1 Vacant possession / Vacant
Bienes mostrencos / Bienes vacantes / Cosas de nadie (E)

Vacant possession property is property with no one in occupation or possession. A property for owner-occupation is generally sold with the benefit of vacant possession. In other words, the present owner will ensure their own or other occupier's removal on or before completion of the sale and leave the property vacant.

1.W.1 Waste (Abuse)

Droit de disposer/Abus (F); Abuso (E)

The doctrine of waste, technically refers to the owner's right to change the nature of the land, whether for better or for worse, although the most common interpretation is of abuse of the land.

Under English Common Law, those with restricted interests in the land such as tenants under a lease, are liable for waste. The owner's interests are usually protected directly by specific covenants in the lease contract.

1.W.2 Wayleave

A wayleave is the right acquired in order to route something through the land of another.

The term is commonly used in respect of gas and other pipelines and electricity and other cables. In legal terms a wayleave is in effect an easement.

REFERENCES CHAPTER 1

BRUCE, J.W., and MIGOT-ADHOLLA, S., *Introduction : Are Indigenous African Tenure Systems Insecure ?* in BRUCE, J.W., and MIGOT-ADHOLLA, S.,*Searching for Land Tenure Security in Africa*, Kendall/Hunt Publishing Co, Iowa, 1994

CARD, R., MURDOCH, J., SCHOFIELD, P., *Law for Estate Management Students*, 4th Ed, Butterworths, London, 1994

FIG, *The FIG Statement on the Cadastre*, International Federation of Surveyors, Australia, 1995

THOMAS, P., *Western Samoa : Custom, change and constraints in relation to land rights, registration and productivity*, in ACQUAYE, B., and CROCOMBE, R., Eds., *Land Tenure and Rural Productivity in the Pacific Islands*, University of the South Pacific, Suva, Fiji Islands, 1984

WAITANGI TRIBUNAL, *Maoriwhenua Fishing Report : Report of the Waitangi Tribunal on the Maoriwhenua Fishing Claim*, Department of Justice, Wellington, New Zealand, 1988

WEIBE, K., TEGENE, A., KUHN, B., *Partial Interests in Land : Policy Tools for Resource Use and Conservation*, US Department of Agriculture, Economic Research Service, Agricultural Economic Report No 744, Washington, 1996

II. ELEMENTAL DESCRIPTIONS
OF SPACE

CHAPTER 2

Elemental descriptions of space

2.A.1 Agrarian

Agraire (F); Agrario (E)

Agrarian is almost synonymous with the term "agricultural" in the English language. An agrarian society is one in which agriculture plays a large role in defining economic, political and cultural values.

Agrarian has strong overtones relating it to land ownership, but it is not exclusively concerned with land issues. Agrarian reform includes reforms to the production structure, the service structure and the land tenure system. Such reforms are often redistributive and are invariably politically contentious.

2.A.2 Airspace

Airspace is the area above the physical surface of the earth.

The possession of land brings with it the possession of the surface, together in principle in some jurisdictions that derive their legal philosophy from English land law with all that is beneath the surface and the column of airspace above. Some jurisdictions restrict these rights. Any use of the defined airspace unauthorised by the possessor is a trespass. This would include projections from neighbouring buildings or structures. Flight over the land would generally not give rise to a trespass, as long as the flying height was reasonable in the context of current wind and weather conditions.

2.A.3 Area

Espace (F); Espacio (E)

Area is the measurement of a specified physical surface of an object. In the context of land it is usually defined as within delineated boundaries and expressed in measures, such as hectares, acres or parts thereof. With buildings it should be defined specifically according to the purpose, for example, whether for insurance or for rental assessment. The measurement of the area will be expressed in measures, such as square metres or square feet.

2.B.1 Brownfield sites

Brownfield sites are potential development sites that involve the redevelopment of urban land.

They are frequently found in areas of existing towns and cities where changes and transfers in technology have altered transportation methods and the locations of industrial processes. Common areas subject to brownfeld site redevelopment are port and harbour areas. Formerly extensive docking, warehousing and accommodation facilities have been rendered largely redundant by the development of large scale container-based transportation which has involved relocation of port facilities to sites with more appropriate land and sea access.

Although the development of such sites is often viewed as politically, economically and environmentally desirable, they often pose significant problems for developers. These may range from the need to change the public perception of the desirability of the area, through reorientation of transportation links between the brownfield area and other urban areas, to requirements to deal with issues of contaminated land. Development of greenfield sites that are previously undeveloped does not pose the same difficulties, although it does involve the conversion and loss of agricultural land.

2.C.1 Coastal zone

The coastal zone is the zone of transition from land to sea in physical, legal and usually land ownership terms. It is a complex area of particular administrative and planning concern.

There is no standard definition of what a coastal zone is. Although there is an understanding of what it constitutes, precise boundaries used vary between jurisdictions and for different purposes. A longstanding and practical definition is "... the part of the land affected by its proximity to the sea and that part of the sea affected by its proximity to the land as the extent to which man's land-based activities have a measurable influence on water chemistry and marine ecology." USCMSER, 1969. Characteristic problems in this area include coastal erosion, habitat loss and degradation, contamination and coastal pollution. As a result many jurisdictions deal specifically with the issues of the coastal zone. STANNERS, D., and BORDEAU, P., 1995

2.C.2 Communal territory
Finage (F)

The concept of communal territory is principally related to agrarian economies based on peasant agriculture where there has been a strong identification of the land within a commune's area with the peasants of the commune working that land. (The commune is the smallest administrative district in several countries, especially in Europe.)
In fact, even in such circumstances in the agricultural areas of France it is becoming increasingly difficult to make any meaningful observations because the land administratively identified as that of the commune often no longer coincides with the agricultural areas worked by the inhabitants. It is not a term that has any specific meaning in the context of England and Wales.

2.C.3 Conservation areas

A conservation area is an area, usually designated under a planning system, where conservation of existing characteristics is given a strong weighting in development decisions.

A conservation area is a planning designation introduced under the Civic Amenities Act, 1967, in ***England and Wales*** *for areas of architectural or historical importance in built-up areas. The designation gives an element of protection to the whole area from unsympathetic development. It recognises that it is frequently the overall assembly of buildings, rather than their individual qualities, that make an area culturally important. These designations therefore fulfil a different function than the protection of listed buildings. Local authorities can designate such areas using their protective powers under the act to preserve and enhance an area*

IMAGE 2

2.C.1 Coastal zone

A coastal zone in Sri Lanka, south of Colombo. C. Sanchez, FAO photo.

2.C.4 Convention sites

Convention sites are conservation areas established following international conventions to conserve the features identified in the specific convention.

Examples of international conventions resulting in the designation of specific sites for nature conservation include:
Ramsar Convention: *The Convention on Wetlands of International Importance, 1971 (named after the Iranian city hosting the convention) is a global agreement for the protection of wetland sites in the around 70 signatory countries. The convention is backed by the International Union for the Conservation of Nature and the International Wildfowl and Wetlands Research Bureau. The total area of sites designated globally is around 36 million hectares. In the UK for example there are 57 sites totalling 215,000 hectares. The Ramsar Convention achieves its aims by monitoring wetlands and assisting in their conservation, by provision of detailed guidance on making rational use of the natural resource, and assistance with financial support to developing countries through a fund set up in 1990.*

Examples of international conventions resulting in the designation of specific sites for heritage conservation include:
World Heritage Convention: *This 1972 convention is supported by UNESCO and aims to designate sites of outstanding universal value, both natural and cultural. At present in Europe for example there are around 20 natural and 120 cultural sites on the list.*

2.D.1 Domain / Estates / Property
Domaine / Propriété (F); Dominio (E)

Under the French Civil Code, and in countries influenced by French legal development a distinction is drawn between the public and private estates.

In other countries, contrasts can be drawn between the public domain (public lands, or land held by the state), and private domain.

2.E.1 Eminent domain

Domaine éminent (F)

The term "eminent domain" is used in some jurisdictions, such as the United States, to describe the process of compulsory acquisition or expropriation. The term derives from the state's position as having ultimate power over the land.

2.E.2 Environmentally designated areas

An environmentally designated area is designated under a planning system to enjoy increased protection against development.

Most countries employ a range of different legislatively defined designations to provide protection to areas that are of particular environmental importance. There are often international designations for the most important sites overlaying the national hierarchy of protected sites.

2.F.1 Foreshore

The foreshore is the area between high water and low water mark.

In jurisdictions with law derived from English law, the foreshore commonly identifies an area of specific, frequently state, ownership, although this is not always the case.

2.G.1 Greenfield sites

The term greenfield site is used in respect of potential development sites that involve the development of agricultural or undeveloped land.

Development of greenfield sites that are previously undeveloped does not pose the same technical development difficulties as "brownfield" development, although it does involve the conversion and loss of agricultural land.

2.H.1 High water mark

The high water mark is the line of the highest tide and is often used legally to define the seaward limit of ownership of land in jurisdictions derived from English common law, although this is not always the case.

2.L.1 Landscape
Paysage (F); Paisaje (E)

The landscape is a product of the interaction of human beings with the natural environment often over a period of many centuries. The landscape therefore reflects the impacts of social, economic and political changes on the natural environment.

2.L.2 Low water mark

The low water mark is the lowest mark that the tide regularly reaches. The low water mark is the seaward boundary of the foreshore and in many cases in jurisdictions derived from English common law delimits both an ownership boundary and the seaward boundary of planning jurisdictions.

2.M.1 Marine park

Marine parks are statutorily designated and protected marine areas of high conservation value where conservation is promoted particularly through controlled use and access. Marine parks are generally established with similar aims of conservation and public access to those applied in conventional land-based national parks.

Examples of an internationally known marine park include:
Great Barrier Reef, Australia: *The Great Barrier Reef Marine Park Authority operates through a comprehensive system of zoning plans covering its designated area and identifying appropriate uses for mapped zones. The zoning provisions assume that the Park is to be conserved as a multiple use resource and cover a wide range of permitted activities. The broadest definition of these is found in the*

general use zones in which reasonable uses consistent with conservation of the reef are allowed. The zones become progressively more restrictive with defined protective marine national park zones and scientific research and preservation zones. The latter is the most restrictive of the zones identified, preventing use and entry of both the marine space and the first 500 feet of air space without the required permit.

2.N.1 National domain / State land / Public lands
Biens domaniaux / Domaine national / Domaine foncier national (F); Bienes fiscales / Dominio nacional / Dominio de tierras nacionales (E)

State land in some jurisdictions is a distinct class of land owned by the state.

2.N.2 National / regional park
Parc national ou régional (F); Parque nacional (E)

National parks are statutorily designated and protected areas of high conservation value where conservation is promoted particularly through controlled use and access. National parks fall within the IUCN definition of protected areas managed mainly for ecosystem protection and recreation.

> Natural area of land and/or sea, designated to
> protect the ecological integrity of one or more ecosystems for present and future generations,
> exclude exploitation or occupation inimical to the purposes of designation of the area and
> provide a foundation for spiritual, scientific, educational, recreational and visitor opportunities, all of which must be environmentally and culturally compatible. IUCN, 1994.

Regional parks are usually of more limited conservation value and are often designated more as small scale recreational reserves. The conception of national parks and regional parks differs significantly as between one another, and as between different jurisdictions. They tend to have in common the aims to conserve areas of land from development and to provide access to land for the public.

IMAGE 3

2.N.2 National / regional park

Zebra near the gates of Lake Mburo National park, midway between Masaka and Mbarara in western Uganda.

K. Dunn, FAO photo.

2.O.1 Open space / Green belt

Espace vert (F); Espacio verde / Área verde (E)

Land designated as "green belt" is land that is protected by town planning against urban development. It is generally found on the urban periphery and was intended to reduce or prevent urban sprawl.

2.P.1 Peri-urban area

Espace périurbain (F); Espacio periurbano (E)

A peri-urban area is an area on the periphery of the urban area of the town and its suburbs.

The peri-urban area is typically very dynamic and is under the most pressure for transformation of greenfield sites into developed urban areas. Planning systems often try to limit the free spread of urban development to reduce the conversion of agricultural land into non-agricultural use and to encourage the efficient use of urban space. These aims are usually supplemented by a range of other initiatives. These include, for example, the designation of green belts to reduce development on urban fringes, and the planning and creation of new towns to try to divert development pressure from existing towns.

Periurban areas in developing countries are very commonly the sites of unregulated and extensive settlement by squatter households moving from rural to urban and from small to large urban areas. Policies for upgrading these areas are a major challenge in development.

2.R.1 Rural / urban

Rural / urbain (F); Rural-urbano / Rurbano / Rururbano / Rurbanización / Rururbanización (E)

The terms rural and urban have their own individual meanings. Rural relates to the countryside and includes typically agricultural and forested areas and landscapes. Urban areas relate to settlements with their characteristic concentrations of residential, commercial and industrial developed property.

In practice these distinctions are less absolute than might be supposed from such definitions. Rural areas also contain settlements, commercial and industrial properties and uses. Urban areas may well contain typically agricultural and forestry related properties and uses. Small "urban farms" are often found in cities in developed countries, and small scale agriculture is a common feature in cities in developing countries.

2.S.1 Seabed

The seabed is the bed of the sea below low water mark. It is to the seaward side of the foreshore. It is very commonly in the exclusive ownership of the state.

2.S.2 State land regime

Domanial / régime domanial (F)

The state land regime is the legislative framework that defines how state land can be allocated and managed.

The legal regime governing state land will cover specific aspects of its management and mode of exploitation. This may include defining the organisation responsible for managing the land, and stating the general principles, and in some cases the detailed basis for its use.

2.T.1 Territorial sea

Mar territorial (F)

The territorial sea includes the area from the high water mark out to 12 nautical miles from the shore baseline over which the coastal state has sovereignty of the territorial sea and the seabed, including the airspace above.

2.T.2 **Territory**
Territoire (F); Entidad territorial / Territorio (E)

Territory may be viewed in legal, social and cultural contexts as the area where an individual or community lives.

It is generally contended that human beings are territorial, and that territoriality is therefore an innate characteristic of individual and social organisation. In practical terms territoriality is expressed in the different forms of property ownership enjoyed by individuals and groups, and by the different ways in which the use of real estate is regulated at different levels of social and political organisation.

Territory ranges from the level of the state, where the state's territory includes all of those areas on land and sea where the state has jurisdiction, through the intermediate levels of local government where democratic responsibility ensures a dimension of social accountability within the relevant administrative boundaries. At the lowest level, each individual will identify an element of personal territory.

Territory is distinguished from the concept of space by this social dimension.

2.T.3 **Town / Urban planning**
Urbanisme (F); Urbanismo (E)

Town planning is the planning framework within which decisions are made about how urban land is to be used.

Town planning is often used as shorthand to denote the statutory planning of land use. The statutory planning of land use, whether urban or rural, whether town planning or rural land management, is based on the principle of rationality, the balancing of conflicting claims on the use of resources taking a comprehensive view of the matters to be taken into account.

2.U.1 Urbanization

Urbanisation (F); Urbanización (E)

Urbanization is the process of development of towns and cities where population growth and population drift typically result in rapid acceleration in the size of the urbanized population.

2.Z.1 Zoning

Zones / Zonage (F); Zona / Zonificación (F)

Zoning is a planning procedure where a designated zone is allocated for a specified use or uses.

Zoning is a commonly used approach to planning which identifies the uses to which the zoned land may be put and specifies the type, amount and location of that development. It is planned to promote orderly development and to reduce or avoid inconsistent uses adjacent to one another.

REFERENCES CHAPTER 2

IUCN, *Guidelines for Protected Areas Management Categories.* IUCN, Cambridge, UK and Gland, Switzerland, 1994

STANNERS, D., and BORDEAU, P., *Europe's Assessment: the Dobris Assessment*, European Environment Agency, Copenhagen, 1995

USCMSER (US COMMISSION ON MARINE SCIENCE, ENGINEERING AND RESOURCES), *Our Nation and the Sea*, US Govt Printing Office, Washington DC, 1969

III. POLITICAL, PROCEDURAL AND PRACTICAL TOOLS/TERMS OF THE LAND

CHAPTER 3

Political, procedural and practical tools/terms of the land

3.A.1 Aerial photography

Photographie aérienne (F); Fotografía aérea (E)

Aerial photography is the process of photographing the earth's surface from the air, usually from a specially fitted aircraft using high precision photographic equipment.

The large majority of topographical maps are based on aerial photography and photogrammetric methods. The height of the aircraft and the characteristics of the camera and film/sensitivity (black and white, colour, infra-red, digital, etc) determine the scale and character of the photograph. The nature of the photograph results in distortion around the edges of photographs which needs to be corrected using appropriate photogrammetric techniques to make maps. Although vertical photography is the most useful in its applications in mapping, non-vertical or oblique photographs may also be useful for other purposes, including for recording the condition of specific objects or areas.
As with a map, an aerial photograph is an historical document, recording characteristics of the subject area at a specific time. The technique is valuable not just for conventional topographic mapping, it is also used for a wide range of activities and surveys including for scientific research, archaeology, the environment, vegetation cover, and land management. For certain functions it may be necessary to conduct ground surveys in photographed areas for ground referencing of particular characteristics. DALE, P. F., and MCLAUGHLIN, J., 1990

3.A.2 Agrarian reform

Réforme agraire (F); Reforma agraria (E)

An agrarian reform is a collection of activities and changes designed to alter the agrarian structure of a country and the ways of using the land

It invariably has political, economic and soci l / cultural dimensions. The objectives of an agrarian reform are generally to improve both qualitatively and quantitatively the levels of agricultural production and to improve the standards of living of agricultural producers. Such reforms will often involve elements of redistribution of land and changes to the land tenure system.

3.B.1 Boundary marking

Bornage (F); Deslinde / Amojonamiento (E)

Boundary marking is an operation that consists of fixing the boundaries of a parcel of land.

"Most parcel boundaries are defined by stable marks or visible features on the ground, which can be natural or artificial. They can be represented by lines on maps, often described by bearings or azimuths and distances, or by coordinates. If the representation on the map has legal priority over the marks on the ground in cases of dispute, the demands for survey accuracy are usually higher than if the case is the opposite. Physical demarcation on the ground is important because it provides actual notice of the boundaries to the landowners." FIG, 1995

In many countries, and for the fixing to have legal validity, the boundary marking must be done by a qualified surveyor.

In situations where systematic registration is taking place, the process of boundary fixing will involve adjudication. Where agreement cannot be reached the decision on boundaries will usually be referred to the courts

3.B.2 Building regulations approval

Permis de construire (aménagement) (F)

Building regulations approval is the process of approving the construction quality of proposed constructions and of their execution.

3.C.1 Charter

Charte (F); Carta (E)

A charter is a formal and fundamental statement at a governmental or inter-governmental level.

Historically the term charter was reserved for a grant or agreement between a monarch and a representation from the subjects. Perhaps the best known charter in English history is the Magna Carta, 1215. This charter is viewed as an important document defining the English constitution, provided significant restrictions on the power of the king and included guarantees of the right to trial for all freemen and justice for everyone.

Charters more recently continue to have some relevance for land related issues. The Royal Institution of Chartered Surveyors (RICS) for example, the professional body under which all qualified "Chartered Surveyors" practise, is enabled by the grant of a Royal Charter from the Queen's Privy Council.

There are other charters of significance that may provide an opportunity for the defence of property as a fundamental human right. The European Charter of Human Rights, judicially administered by the European Court of Human Rights, for example, periodically hears appeals against national legislatures and judiciaries on property related issues.

3.C.2 Code

Code (F); Código (E)

A code is a coherent body of law which pulls together all of the laws relating to a specific field.

It is a common approach to law making in many countries influenced by Roman law, including for example those influenced by the French legal system. Codification has been a particular feature of the law since the Code Napoleon, the first modern codification of French law, was introduced between 1804 and 1810. Codification of laws is also, for example, a common feature of the former Soviet Union republics where, in some cases, developing an effective Land Code has been an important priority.

The terms code and codification are not characteristic of the legal system in the United Kingdom, although it is an approach used to a greater or lesser extent in several states influenced by English law. In English law it is reasonably common, however, for "consolidating laws" to be passed. Although not the same as codification, such laws bring together in one place all of the legislation dealing with a particular issue rather than materially changing the law.

3.C.3 Codification

Codification (F); Codificación (E)

The process of codification is the development of a coherent legal code from an existing body of law.

3.C.4 Compulsory acquisition / expropriation

Expropriation / expropriation pour cause d'utilité publique (F); Expropiación/ Expropiación por causa de utilidad pública (E)

Compulsory acquisition or expropriation is a procedure by which public needs for land or property rights in the pursuit of government policy are met.

Processes of compulsory acquisition and needs vary from country to country. The processes of acquisition are statutorily defined, and will include detailed requirements and timetables for procedures and notices on the part of both parties. The processes will also include a basis for setting compensation for the loss of the owner expropriated.

Common requirements for the compulsory acquisition of land include for public infrastructure such as construction of roads and railways, for easements for power cables and pipelines, for hospitals, schools and public housing. In some countries, it may also for example form a part of land reform policy to compulsorily acquire land for redistribution.

The philosophical justification for the compulsory acquisition of land is that the private owner of land enjoys the benefits of living in society.

The owner accordingly should accept that if the public can legally establish a need for the land then it should be entitled to acquire the land in return for appropriate compensation. The issue of compensation and the right of citizens not to be arbitrarily deprived of their property is one that is often dealt with in principle in national constitutions.

The equivalent of compulsory purchase in England and Wales, is "expropriation" in continental Europe, "taking" in North America, and "resumption" in Australia.

3.C.5 Conservation management

Gestion patrimoniale (F)

Conservation management is an extension of land management that emphasises the need to protect and safeguard natural resources.

Conservation management may take a wide variety of forms, although it is increasingly widespread for there to be a strong element of local, or decentralised, input into implementation. The need for this has been repeatedly emphasised in UN conferences starting with the Rio Summit in 1992, and has been taken up by communities around the world.

3.D.1 Decentralisation

Décentralisation (F); Decentralización / Decentralización de los procesos administrativos (F)

Decentralisation is a process of moving from the centre to the periphery. In governmental terms decentralisation is likely to involve the shifting of decision-making and executive powers to lower tiers of government and particularly to local government.

Decentralisation has become a significant issue of policy particularly since the 1980's when the World Commission on Environment and Development laid emphasis on the importance of bringing environmental and economic issues more effectively into decision-making. This emphasis on local responsibility has been repeated through successive UN conferences starting from the Rio Summit in 1992.

3.D.2 Development plan

Development plans identify proposed land uses adopted by the relevant planning authority in a given area. They are usually associated with urban or town and country planning.

3.G.1 General development order

A general development order identifies permitted development in a town and country planning system.

> *The general development order (GDO) is a provision in the planning system in the United Kingdom under the Town and Country Planning Acts to identify those developments that do not require planning permission, although they may require building regulation approval and listed building consent depending on circumstances.*
>
> *The function of the GDO is to define a class of "permitted development". This takes out of the development control system those actions that would come within the definition of development under the Act, but which are effectively marginal.*

3.G.2 Geomatics
Géomatique (F); Geomática (E)

Geomatics is commonly defined as a 'discipline aimed at managing geographic data by means of the science and technology used to acquire, store, process, display and distribute them.' (Canadian Institute of Geomatics – the first professional institution to make the change from, in this case, Surveying and Mapping.)

It is " … a field of activities which, using a systemic approach, integrates all the means used to acquire and manage spatial data required as part of scientific, administrative, legal and technical operations involved in the process of the production and management of spatial information. These activities include, but are not limited to, cartography, control surveying, engineering surveying, geodesy, hydrography, land information management, land surveying, mining surveying, photogrammetry and remote sensing. "WILLIAMSON, I., P., et al., 1994

3.G.3 GIS (Geographical Information System)

SIG (Système d'Information Géographique) (F);
Sistema de Información Geográfica (SIG) (E)

GIS is: "... a set of computer tools for collecting, storing, retrieving at will, transforming, and displaying spatial data ..." The development of computers and appropriate software has enabled maps to be transformed from a static past to a dynamic future. The uses to which GIS can be put reflect its capacity to model the real world and for the constituent data to be selected, interrelated, analysed and used for a specific set of purposes.
BURROUGH, P. A., and MCDONNELL, R. A., 1998

3.G.4 GPS (Global Positioning System)

GPS (Système de positionnement universel) (F);
Sistema de posicionamiento por satélite (GPS) (E)

The global positioning system consists of 24 satellites orbiting the earth in six orbital planes. Locations on the ground can be fixed and their coordinates calculated on the basis of signals picked up from these satellites by receivers. The high degree of accuracy and consistency of measurements using this positioning capability make it an excellent option for almost all types of geodesy and surveying, including cadastral work. UNECE, 1996

3.I.1 Integrated coastal zone management

The complexities and frequent overlaps of the processes, ownership, and administrative structures in coastal zones, coupled with their physical and environmental fragility, have led to the common recognition that they require careful integrated planning, referred to as integrated coastal zone management.

IMAGE 4

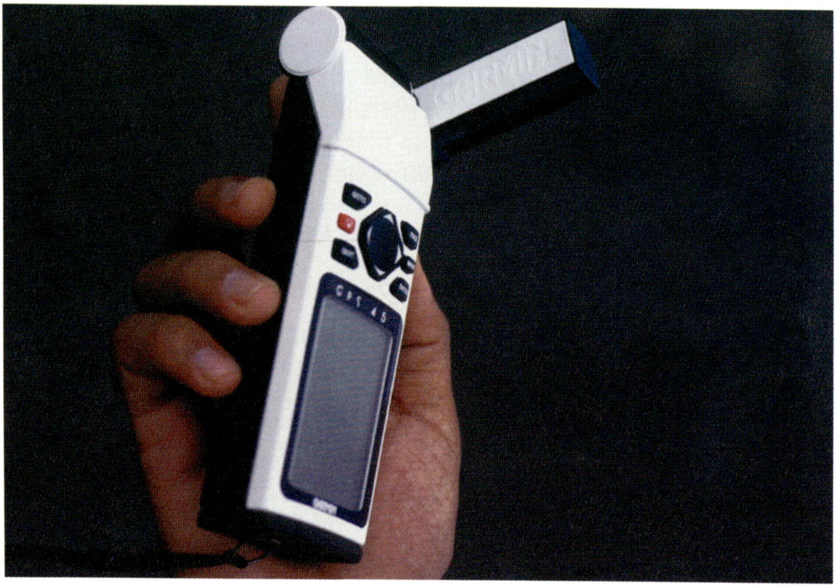

3.G.4 GPS (Global Positioning System)

A Global Positioning System, an instrument to determine the precise location of locust's infestation. This information is transmitted to a centre in Tulear, Malagasy, which then organizes their elimination.

A. Proto, FAO photo.

3.L.1 Land consolidation

Remembrement (F); Concentración parcelaria (E)

Land consolidation is a sequence of operations designed to reorganise land parcels in an area, regrouping them into consolidated holdings of more regular form and with improved access.

Consolidation of parcels of land into a single holding, whether voluntary or enforced, is intended to provide a more rational distribution of land to improve the efficiency of farming. Each agricultural enterprise, consisting prior to the consolidation of many parcels spread over a wide area, will consist afterwards of a small number or perhaps a single parcel. Land consolidation operates on the basis of assessing the quality of land and providing owners with equivalent land in exchange. Once the consolidation scheme is agreed, the proposals are made available to the public for a period of notice to enable any appeals to be made. The consolidation process should not therefore affect the size or number of agricultural enterprises. UNECE, 1996

Land consolidation schemes are increasingly associated with other improvements, for example, highway and access road layouts, removal of hedgerows, drainage or irrigation systems, and wildlife and conservation projects.

3.L.2 Land development

Land development is the application of resources to improve land that should enable it to be used more efficiently. These resources may include capital (constructing buildings), labour (clearing or draining land for agriculture) or enterprise (securing or revising planning permissions).

Land development is a facet of land management, and applies to both rural and urban land. Development may result in increased value of the land, and where properly managed will release an element of development value enabling the developer to recoup investment and other costs and make a profit. In some circumstances this may be referred to as betterment and may be subject to a special tax.
This is distinct from the French use of the term "amenagement foncier" now based on the "droit de l'amenagement foncier rural" which aims to

improve farm working conditions and productivity and is integrated with urban planning schemes in mixed farmland and urban development land reallocations. LORVELLEC, L., 1992

3.L.3 Land management

Gestion de terroir (F);
Decentralización de la gestión territorial (E)

Land management is identified by the International Federation of Surveyors as follows: "Land management is the process of managing the use and development of land resources. Some of the critical, and sometimes conflicting, objectives that must be addressed by land management policies today include:

> improving the efficiency of land resource use to support the rapidly growing population of many countries;
> providing incentives for development, including the provision of residential housing and basic infrastructure such as sewer and water facilities;
> protecting the natural environment from degradation;
> providing equitable and efficient access to the economic benefits of land and real estate markets;
> supporting government services through taxation and fees related to land and improvements." FIG, 1991

Land management is distinct from farm management. The latter deals with issues such as what to produce, how much to produce and how to produce. The land manager, on the other hand, focuses on the management of the land, whether urban or rural. Land management in its broadest sense deals, therefore, with issues relating to:

> the achievement of an acceptable return from the land interests owned.
> the maintenance or enhancement of the value of the land interests owned.
> such returns and values are likely to include a mixture of financial/economic, social and environmental (including sustainability) qualities.

NIX, J., HILL, P., WILLIAMS, N., and BAUGH, J., 1998

The land manager is the person undertaking such management, whether as an owner or agent, and whether in the public or the private sector. This area of land management is often referred to in United Kingdom practice as estate management.

3.L.4 Land policy

Politique foncière (F); Política agraria (E)

Land policy is the set of intentions embodied in various policy instruments that are adopted by the state to organise land tenure and land use.
Land policy will usually be guided by a set of basic principles, some of which owe their origin to international agreements, others to specific national circumstances. These principles may include:

> encouragement of efficiency and promotion of economic development
> promotion of equality and social justice
> preservation of the environment and sustainable patterns of land use GTZ, 1998

Not all countries have a coherent, consciously integrated and formally stated land policy.

3.L.5 Land reform

Réforme foncière (F); Reforma agraria (E)

Land reform is the generic term for modifications in the legal and institutional framework governing land policy. Land reform is intended to implement changes in land policy that are designed to realise desired changes in a changing political, economic and social environment. The most common types of land reform are probably those dealing with reallocations of land and those redistributing legal rights of ownership. Land reform is invariably a part of agrarian reform. There is a common perception that land reform is the prerogative of developing and transforming economies. The reality is that land policy and the legislative and institutional framework implementing that policy are constantly changing in all societies as political, economic and social circumstances change.

3.L.6 Land system
Système foncier (F); Sistema de tierras (E)

"Land system" is synonymous with "land tenure system". It provides the basis for access to land and natural resources. It defines the ways in which land and natural resources can be held and the security of those rights. The system comprises the legislative and administrative frameworks relating to land and natural resources and to their application.

3.L.7 Land use plan
Plan d'occupation des sols (F);
Plan de ocupación del suelo (E)

Land use planning is "The systematic assessment of land and water potential, alternative patterns of land use and other physical, social and economic conditions, for the purpose of selecting and adopting land use options which are most beneficial to land users without degrading the resources or the environment, together with the selection of measures most likely to encourage such land uses."
CHOUDHURY, K., and JANSEN, L. J. M., 1999

Land use planning in its statutory sense is undertaken under the Town and Country Planning legislation in England and Wales through its structure and local plans. The main focus for this planning is to control the current and future development of the defined areas.

This is distinct from the French approach where around half of the 36,000 French municipalities have formally adopted a zoning map (Plan d'occupation des sols – POS). Under the latter, land is divided into urban districts ("U" zones) and natural districts ("N" zones): NA for future urbanisation, NB with existing settlement frozen, NC with just agricultural use, and ND with environmentally sensitive areas. A local farmers' "parliament" is involved in the drafting prior to final approval by local government. LORVELLEC, L., 1992

The term land use plan is also used in the context of a tool for the management of land within a specific ownership.

3.M.1 Maps / Mapping / Cartography

Carte / Cartographie (F); Mapa / Carta / Generalización cartográfica / Cartografía (E)

Traditionally, maps represent physical, vegetational or political features of a spatially defined area on paper or some other flat medium. Such maps have been a vital part of development and of all aspects of land management and administration since earliest records began. They are, however, relatively static and are difficult to change and update compared with modern digitally based GIS.

3.O.1 Orthophotography

Orthophotographie (F); Ortofoto (E)

Orthophotography is a process that creates undistorted photographic images using stereo pairs of aerial photographs.

Orthophotography has been developed to maximise the potential use and accuracy of aerial photography. It achieves this accuracy by using stereo pairs of photographs mounted in a special machine which enables the distortion that is inherent in aerial photographs to be minimised, maintaining a constant scale across the image. These distortions result from the effects of terrain and the perspective effects inherent in the use of the camera. The digitised image is processed into a particular map projection giving a uniform scale and known accuracy. A mosaic of such photographs is used to build up an orthophotomap. GIS often uses orthophotographs to provide a rich visual context, integrated with other geographic information.
DALE, P. F., and MCLAUGHLIN, J., 1990

3.P.1 Parcel plan / Cadastral plan / Map

Plan parcellaire (F); Plan parcelario / Carta predial (E)

A parcel plan is generally a large scale map of an area showing all of the property parcels and their use, the boundaries and the distances between them and the buildings and improvements. Generally the parcel plan includes a register of the parcels. In the context of land administration, a cadastral plan is a parcel plan. The nearest equivalent in land management in jurisdictions influenced by English practice is termed an estates terrier.

3.P.2 Perimeter / Boundary

Périmètre (F); Perimetro (E)

A perimeter is a boundary.

3.P.3 Photogrammetry

Photogrammétrie (F); Fotogrametría / Restitución (E)

Photogrammetry is the set of measurement techniques by which aerial photographs, converted into orthophotographs, are analysed and converted into maps and geographical information.

Photogrammetry measures position and altitude from stereo aerial photographs or images using a stereoscope or stereoplotter.

3.P.4 Photomapping

Photomapping is the analysis of aerial photographs to provide the information for creating maps and geographical information.

This is generally undertaken by assembling orthophotographs from stereo pairs of aerial photographs, and using photogrammetric techniques to create the maps.

3.P.5 Photoplan / Orthophotoplan

Photoplan / Orthophotoplan (F); Fotomapa (E)

A photoplan is an assembly of enlarged aerial photographs. An orthophotoplan is an accurately scaled photoplan that has had any distortions corrected.

An orthophotoplan is made by assembling accurately positioned and geometrically corrected aerial photographs. An orthophotoplan has the characteristics of a map, with orientation, a scale and a key to identify relevant features. It combines the accuracy of a map with the ease of understanding of a photograph.

3.P.6 Plan

Plan (F); Plano (E)

A plan is a representation of an object in a horizontal projection, for example, of a building or group of buildings, of a farm, or of a land parcel.

A plan is also used in a town and country, or other planning context. Local plans in England and Wales, for example, are based on a large scale map, usually with a descriptive statement of the planning policies for a given area. A plan differs from a map typically in its scale.

3.R.1 Regularisation of ownership / Formalisation of ownership

Régularisation foncière (F); Regularización de tierras (E)

Regularisation of ownership is where informal or illegal occupation of land is legalised by statute, giving occupiers the legal right to private ownership of the land.

Regularisation of ownership usually occurs where there has been a large amount of irregular settlement, and there is a need to preserve the investments made by the illegal occupiers. It is therefore a policy that retains the population in place and minimises displacement. The approach favours the rehabilitation and integration of an illegal settlement rather than its systematic destruction. This results from the size of these illegal settlements and because governments can neither afford the financial costs of the classical solution of resettlement, nor the political cost of destruction of the illegal settlements.

3.R.2 Remote sensing

Télédétection (F); Teledetección / Percepción remota (E)

Remote sensing is the set of techniques used for gathering information about the environment without being in direct contact with it.

These techniques extend human perception by recording in different ways the radiation emitted or reflected by objects, and using the characteristic radiation patterns of individual objects that enable their identification. Remote sensing techniques are extensively used to record physical and biological characteristics of objects as the basis for thematic mapping and for measuring change. These include for the mapping of urban, agricultural, forestry and aquatic themes. Remote sensing techniques are particularly closely associated with satellite imagery range but also range from aerial photography, through radar, to sonar. DALE, P. F., and MCLAUGHLIN, J., 1990

3.R.3 Reserve / Land reserve / Nature reserve

Réserve / réserve foncière / Réserve naturelle (F);
Reserva de bienes raíces / Reserva natural (E)

The word reserve signifies a defined area of land set aside for a particular purpose. The term is commonly used in the following contexts:

> reserve land: land reserves may be identified and set aside for specified public purposes in some jurisdictions

> nature reserve: land may be designated and set aside as a nature reserve for the purposes of protection of valued fauna and flora

> native reserve: land may be designated and set aside for the exclusive use of indigenous peoples

Examples of the use of the term "reserve" in the context of reserve land include:
Malaysia: *Article 62 of the National Land Code empowers the State Authority to gazette any state land as reserved for any public purpose. The land reserved cannot thereafter be disposed of by the state, and cannot be used for any other purpose than that which it was reserved for.*
Examples of the use of the term "reserve" in the context of native reserve include:
Fiji: *Around 88% of Fiji's land is held under customary tenure by the indigenous Fijian people. Native land is inalienable and is categorised according to whether or not the land is in native reserve. Land is leased through the Native Land Trust Board which administers land under a statutory trust. Leasing of native reserve land is restricted principally to indigenous Fijians. Native land which is not leased is used by the owners following customary practices.*

IMAGE 5

3.R.2 Remote sensing

FAO expert discusses mapping and analysis of remote sensing data. Students are learning to use a mirror stereoscope (left) for aerial photos, and a stereopret (right), an instrument for topographical and contour-mapping use

I. de Borhegyi, FAO photo.

3.R.4 Right of abode

Permis d'habiter (F); Permiso para habitar un lugar (E)

A right of abode is an administrative authorisation given by the municipal or local authority to the occupier of an area, restricting the right of abode to that area.

3.S.1 Scale

Échelle (F); Escala (E)

The scale is the relationship between the representation of an object on a plan or map, and its size in reality. A graphic scale is a graduated line, divided into equal sections, indicating the relation between the distances marked on the map or plan and the distances in reality.
A numerical scale is the mathematical relation between a distance on the plan or map and in reality, for example 1mm on the map represents 100m in reality at a scale of 1:100,000. Scales are classified into three categories. Large scales are those up to 1:25,000; medium scales are between 1:25,000 and 1: 100,000; small scales are those in excess of 1:100,000. The more detailed a map, the larger its scale.

3.S.2 Secure tenure

Sécurisation foncière (F);
Legalización y reconocimiento de la posesión de tierras (E)

Secure tenure is related to the degree of recognition and guarantee of real estate rights.
Improving security of tenure is seen as necessary:

> to encourage investments to improve the productivity of agriculture;
> for conservation and the sound use of natural resources;
> to encourage the use of temporary rights for the use of land including leasing
> to reduce the number and the intensity of conflicts relating to the use and transaction of real estate.

Conversely, insecurity of tenure is characterised when the users and holders of land, whether rural or urban, consider that their rights on the land are at risk to other actors and uncertain in their duration.

3.S.3 Structure plan

Structure plans are plans developed by planning authorities to provide a strategic policy framework for local planning and development control.

3.S.4 Subdivision / Mutation

Subdivision is the process of demarcation of parcels when an area of land is divided.

> *The process is closely regulated in many jurisdictions. Examples of subdivision procedures include:*
> ***Malaysia*** *Part 9 of the National Land Code of Malaysia regulates subdivision. It lays down the conditions for approval of a subdivision, including for example that the shape of the parcel should be suitable for the intended purposes in the opinion of the State Director or Land Administrator, and that satisfactory means of access must be available. It also provides for how applications are to be made and what fees are to be levied.*

3.S.5 Surveyor / Land surveyor / Cadasral surveyor

Géomètre (F); Geómetra (E)

A surveyor is defined as follows by the International Federation of Surveyors (FIG):

"A surveyor is a professional person with the academic qualifications and technical expertise to practise the science of measurement; to assemble and assess land and geographic related information; to use that information for the purpose of planning and implementing the efficient administration of the land, the sea and structures thereon; and to instigate the advancement and development of such practices.

"Practice of the surveyor's profession may involve one or more of the following activities which occur either on, above or below the surface of the land or sea and may be carried out in association with other professionals.

1 The determination of the size and shape of the earth and the measurement of all data needed to define the size, position, shape and contour of any part of the earth's surface.
2 The positioning of objects in space and the positioning and monitoring of physical features, structures and engineering works on, above or below the surface of the earth.
3 The determination of the position of the boundaries of public or private land, including national and international boundaries, and the registration of those lands with the appropriate authorities.
4 The design, establishment and administration of land and geographic information systems and the collection, storage and analysis of data within those systems.
5 The study of the natural and social environment, the measurement of land and marine resources and the use of data in the planning of development in urban, rural and regional areas.
6 The planning, development and redevelopment of property, whether urban or rural and whether land or buildings.
7 The assessment of value and the management of property, whether urban or rural and whether land or buildings.
8 The planning, measurement and management of construction works, including the estimation costs.
9 The production of plans, maps, files, charts and reports.

In the application of the foregoing activities surveyors take into account the relevant legal, economic, environmental and social aspects affecting each project. FIG, 1991

3.T.1 Topography

Topographie (F); Topografía (E)

Topography is the set of methods used to enable the nature of the land to be identified, measured and shown.

The topographic map represents the detailed physical attributes of the area using conventional signs and methods. Height, for example is commonly shown using contours or spot heights, and more rarely, for example, using shading. A topographic map usually uses colours which allows a diversity of topographical features to be shown.

3.T.2 Town and country planning
Urbanisme (F); Urbanismo (E)

Town and country planning is the planning framework within which decisions are made about how land is to be used.

The concept of town and country planning varies between cultures and differs significantly between jurisdictions. There are two significantly different broad approaches. A more flexible system developed in the United Kingdom and has been applied in many of the countries influenced by British legal and administrative systems. This approach seeks to reconcile conflicts in land use and allows both discretion and flexibility in the implementation of planning to try to achieve development that is in the public interest.

This contrasts with the relative inflexibility of the zoning and related systems of planning typically found in United States and continental European jurisdictions which focus principally on the establishment and protection of property rights.

The statutory planning of land use, whether urban or rural, is based on the principle of rationality, the balancing of conflicting claims on the use of resources taking a comprehensive view of the matters to be taken into account.

3.U.1 Urban parcel map / Cadastral map
Parcellaire urbain (F); Parcelario urbano / Carta o mapa catastral / Plano catastral (E)

An urban parcel map is a map identifying the ownership parcels in an urban area.

Urban parcel maps may form the basis of a number of functions including particularly, for example, in relation to real estate taxation and planning.

REFERENCES CHAPTER 3

BURROUGH P.A, McDONNELL R.A, *Principals of Geographical Information Systems*, Oxford University Press, Oxford, 1998.

CULLINGWORTH, J. B., and NADIN, V., *Town and Country Planning in the UK*, Routledge, London, 1997

DALE, P. F., and MCLAUGHLIN, J., *Land Information Management : An Introduction with Special Reference to Cadastral Problems in Third World Countries*, Oxford University Press, Oxford, 1990

FIG (INTERNATIONAL FEDERATION OF SURVEYORS), *The Surveyor's Contribution to Land Management*, FIG, 1991

FIG (INTERNATIONAL FEDERATION OF SURVEYORS), *Definition of a Surveyor*, FIG, 1991

GTZ (Deutsche Gesellschaft für Technische Zusammenarbeit), *Land Tenure in Development Cooperation*, GTZ, Eschborn, Germany, 1998

LORVELLEC, L., *Agrarian Law in France*, in GROSSMAN, M. R., and BRUSSARD, W., *Agrarian Land Law in the Western World*, CAB International, Wallingford, UK, 1992

NIX, J., HILL, P., WILLIAMS, N., and BAUGH, J., *Land and Estate Management*, Packard Publishing, Chichester, UK, 1998

UNECE, *Land Administration Guidelines*, Meeting of Officials in Land Administration, UNECE, Geneva, 1996

WILLIAMSON, I., P., LEAHY, F., J., and HUNTER, G., J., *Education for Surveyors in Australia : a Vision for the 21st Century*, XX Congress, International Federation of Surveyors, Melbourne, 1994

IV. LAND INFORMATION SYSTEMS: SERVICES AND TOOLS OF PUBLIC LAND ADMINISTRATION

CHAPTER 4

Land information systems: services and tools of public land administration

4.A.1 Adjudication

Adjudication is the process of final and authoritative determination of the existing rights and claims of people to land. This may be in the context of first registration of those rights, or it may be to resolve a doubt or dispute after first registration. Adjudication is also a standard procedure prior to the operation of a land consolidation scheme.

The process of adjudication should simply reveal what rights already exist, by whom they are held and what restrictions or limitations there are on them. In practice, of course, the mere fact of a final and definitive recording of these rights is a significant change in those jurisdictions where previously there had been uncertainty.

The process of adjudication may be sporadic or systematic, as with registration. Sporadic adjudication is a parcel by parcel approach, usually triggered by some specific event, like the sale of the property. Depending on the jurisdiction sporadic adjudication will then involve demonstrating that the title is basically sound before it is accepted and entered into the registration system. UNECE, 1996

4.B.1 Boundary / Perimeter

Périmètre (F); Perímetro (E)

The International Federation of Surveyors (FIG) defines boundaries as follows:

"Boundaries of parcels can be defined by physical demarcation on the ground or by a mathematical description usually based on a co-ordinate system. The accuracy and cost of cadastral surveys is dependent on the accuracy needed for boundary descriptions. The accuracy should reflect factors such as the value of the land, the risk and cost of land disputes and the information needs of the users of the cadastre."
FIG, 1991

It is often the case that the boundary will be physically demarcated (e.g., by markers such as pipes, pegs, etc.) even when a jurisdiction uses a coordinate system to describe the position of the boundary. Coordinates tend to refer to physical objects on the ground and not to abstract positions.
A principal difference between boundaries is whether:

> the entire length of a boundary is demarcated by a physical feature (e.g., a river [centre or either bank], ridge, wall, or hedge, etc.)
> only the bend points of the boundary are demarcated by physical points (often referred to as monuments, beacons, etc).

This difference is often raised as the clash between "general" and "fixed" boundaries in a debate that has long plagued the English-speaking community. This debate often ignores the fact that so-called "general" boundaries such as rivers do exist in so-called "fixed" boundary jurisdictions. In one sense, fixed boundaries are no more fixed than general boundaries; they are merely delimited more precisely.

Regardless of the nature of the boundary, the documentation of the boundary position should be sufficient to allow the boundary to be relocated should it somehow be destroyed.

4.C.1 Cadastral administration

Administration du cadastre (F); Administración catastral (E)

The cadastral administration in any given jurisdiction is the organisation (or organisations) responsible for creating, maintaining and dealing with the cadastre.

There is a wide range of experience throughout the world. Although it is most common for the administration to be established and managed by traditional government departments, there are instances where such agencies have become self-financing, such as the Netherlands Kadaster. In some countries cadastral issues are the responsibility of local governments, in others they are national, but may be administered under one or more different ministries. The most common ministries with cadastral responsibilities are probably the Ministries of Justice, of Finance and of Agriculture. MANTHORPE, J., 1997

4.C.2 Cadastral register

Registre cadastral (F); Registro catastral (E)

The term "cadastral register" may include registers for any of the different types of cadastral system identified in the definition of the cadastre.

4.C.3 Cadastre

Cadastre (F); Catastro (E)

The International Federation of Surveyors (FIG) defines the cadastre as follows:

"A cadastre is normally a parcel based and up-to-date land information system containing a record of interests in land (i.e. rights, restrictions and responsibilities). It usually includes a geometric description of land parcels linked to other records describing the nature of the interests, and ownership or control of those interests, and often the value of the parcel and its improvements. It may be established for fiscal purposes (e.g. valuation and equitable taxation), legal purposes (conveyancing), to assist in the management of land and land use (e.g. for planning and other administrative purposes), and enables sustainable development and environmental protection." FIG, 1991

Different countries use the term cadastre differently and this is a cause of real confusion. UNECE, 1996

4.D.1 Decentralised resource management

Instances décentralisées de gestion des resources (F);
Instancias decentralizadas de administración de recursos (E)

Decentralised resource management is the principle of delegating policy-making in resource management to the lowest effective local levels of public authority.

The concept of decentralised resource management is one that has been significantly promoted as a result of the UN Commission on Sustainable Development's Agenda 21, and is being taken up increasingly around the world.

4.D.2 Deeds registration

Deeds registration is a system of proof of property ownership and interests based on the registration of transfer and other deeds.

In an official deeds registration system, a copy of the relevant deed, for example a transfer deed, is deposited in the deed registry. An appropriate entry is then made into the register of the time, date, parties and transaction, as may be required by the particular jurisdiction. The documents generally require to be checked by a notary or an authorised lawyer to assure the validity of the transaction and entry.

This transaction reference, together with the supporting deeds, then provides evidence of the vendor's right to sell the property. The deeds registration system is limited in that it does not provide a guarantee of title. It does not provide the clarity, certainty or guarantee required for an ideal system. All that it typically provides is access into the chain of transactions that can be used to prove title.

4.L.1 Land Book

Registre ou livre foncier (F); Registro (E)

The Land Book system (Grundbuch), most commonly associated with Germany, is a system of title registration that is broadly followed in the German states, in Austria and Hungary and in those regions influenced by their respective former empires. The Grundbuch is under the administrative responsibility of the district judge, and is implemented by a full-time professional registrar. Each folio of the Grundbuch, as found in Bavaria, for example, consists of four parts, comprising respectively a description of the property, the name of the proprietor and how the parcel was acquired, details of any servitudes, and, finally, details of any charges such as mortgages. ROWTON SIMPSON, S., 1976

4.L.2 Land certificate

A land certificate is a certified copy of an entry in a land title system and provides proof of the ownership and of encumbrances on the land at that time.

4.L.3 Land charge

A land charge is a right in respect of land.

> *A land charge is registrable in England and Wales under the Land Charges Act, 1972. This is intended to reduce the number of interests affecting the land which would otherwise fall out of the registration system. The charges that are registrable include:*
>
> \> *puisne mortagages (generally second and subsequent legal mortgages which cannot be protected by deposit of the title deeds because the first mortgage is secured by this right) and equitable mortgages (failing to comply with the legal formalities for creating a mortgage)*
> \> *various forms of limited owner's and estate contract interests*
> \> *Inland Revenue charges for inheritance tax*
> \> *restrictive covenants and equitable easements*
> \> *registration of spouse's interests under the Matrimonial Homes Act*
>
> *CARD, R., MURDOCH, J., SCHOFIELD, P., 1994*

4.L.4 Land commissions

Commissions foncières (F); Comisiones de bienes raíces (E)

Land commissions are formally constituted bodies to investigate land related issues, or to implement some aspect of land policy, such as adjudication.

4.L.5 Land dispute

Conflits fonciers (F); Conflictos de tierras / Problema de la tierra (E)

A land dispute is a disagreement over land. A land dispute occurs where specific individual or collective interests relating to land are in conflict.

Land disputes can operate at any scale from the international to those between individual neighbours. At whatever scale, the dispute is likely to owe as much to the general nature of neighbourly relations as to actual problems relating to the land.

Land disputes may arise from a wide range of different situations and are commonly found where there is intense population pressure on land, where different types of land use abut or overlap one another, and where boundaries are not well demarcated. The following are cited as possible causes of land conflicts in HUSSEIN, K., 1998: over access to pastoral resources and damage to crops between herders and farmers; over grazing and watering areas between different groups of herders; where customary boundaries are poorly defined between neighbouring communities; between migrant and indigenous farmers; where expanding cities place pressure on peri-urban areas between the urban elites and peri-urban populations; where population pressure reduces the sizes of holdings below uneconomic levels; and where state allocations of land for forestry or large scale development schemes conflict with customary landholders interests. LEONARD, R., and LONGBOTTOM, J., 2000

Land conflicts may be resolved in a variety of ways. In parts of South Asia, for example, in Sri Lanka, land conflicts may be the subject of court cases that are inherited from generation to generation. In parts of the Highlands of Papua New Guinea, physical conflict between tribes may evidence land conflicts. In parts of Africa the land chief may have an important role in resolving land disputes.

4.L.6 Land Information System (LIS)

Système d'Information Foncière (SIF) (F);
Sistema de información de bienes raíces (E)

Land Information Systems (LIS) have been defined by the International Federation of Surveyors (FIG) as follows:

"... a tool for legal, administrative and economic decision-making and an aid for planning and development. A land information system consists, on the one hand, of a databse containing spatially referenced land-related data for a defined area and, on the other, of procedures and techniques for the systematic collection, updating, processing and distribution of the data. The base of a land information system is a uniform spatial referencing system, which also simplifies the linking of data within the system with other land-related data."
UNECE, 1996

4.L.7 Land register

Registre de la propriété (F); Registro de la propiedad / Certificado de tradición o libertad /Tracto sucesorio o sucesivo (E)

The land register is the definitive record of all registered properties, and comprises the registered details for each property.

In the land register for England and Wales, there are three registers or parts to the register; the Property Register, the Proprietorship Register and the Charges Register. These contain respectively:

> *a clear identification of the parcel and of the right owned, both in the parcel itself and in any other property, including a plan of the parcel*

> *the names of the owners and their addresses, together with any caution or restriction on the owner's right to dispose of the property*

> *any interests adversely affecting the property, including leases, charges, mortgages, restrictive covenants and easements over the property.*

ROWTON SIMPSON, S., 1976

4.L.8 Land registration

The International Federation of Surveyors (FIG) defines land registration as follows: "Land registration is the official recording of legally recognised interests in land and is usually part of a cadastral system. From a legal perspective a distinction can be made between deeds registration, where the documents filed in the registry are the evidence of title, and registration of title, in which the register itself serves as the primary evidence." FIG, 1991 The benefits brought about by instituting a system of land registration need to be viewed in context. "Land registration must be kept in perspective. It is a device which may be essential to sound land administration, but it is merely a part of the machinery of government. It is not some sort of magical specific which will automatically produce good land use and development; nor is it a system of land holding (land tenure); it is not even a kind of land reform, though it may be a valuable administrative aid to land reform. In short, land registration is only a means to an end. It is not an end in itself. Much time, money and effort can be wasted if that elementary truth is forgotten." ROWTON SIMPSON, S., 1976

4.L.9 Land registry / Registration office
Bureau de l'enregistrement des titres (F);
Oficina de registro (E)

The land registry is the institution or office responsible for land registration. The title of the office and the responsibilities vary considerably between jurisdictions, as, accordingly, does the staffing and equipment of the office. Titles of the officer in charge of land registration include:

> Chief Land Registrar (England & Wales, Kenya)
> Keeper of the Registers of Scotland (Scotland)
> Registrar-General of Lands (New Zealand)
> Registrar-General, Registrar of Titles, Commissioner of Titles (variously in the states of Australia)

The responsibilities range from, for example, England & Wales, where the Chief Land Registrar has extensive judicial powers, to Kenya, where applications to resolve or correct problems must be referred to the court in the first instance. ROWTON SIMPSON, S., 1976

4.N.1 Notary
Notaire (F); Notario (E)

The notary is both a conveyancing lawyer and a public official responsible for seeing that the conveyance is properly undertaken.
The notary is a vital part of the system of land transactions in many jurisdictions in continental Europe. It is not a feature of systems of title registration under the Torrens System. The notary is bound by a strict code of ethics, enforced by the relevant national bodies.
ROWTON SIMPSON, S., 1976

4.P.1 Property files / records
Fichier immobilier (F);Fichero inmobiliario/
Archivo inmobiliario / Archivo de la propiedad inmueble (E)

Property files are more associated in an English context with real estate management than with registration activity. In such a context, each property will have on file a documentary record of accounts, correspondence, agreements, contracts and other pertinent matters in relation to its management.

4.P.2 Public access to information

Acceso público a la información (E)

Public access to information is a feature of public policy by which each society defines what information, particularly about private citizens and corporate entities, should be available to the public.

Public access is an important issue in relation to land information as such information can form a very significant part of decision-making for individuals, corporations and governments. It is an area of rapid development as computer and internet technology increase capabilities to access, distribute and analyse data.

Jurisdictions vary in their approaches to the ownership and protection of data within registries. The UNECE Land Administration Guidelines recommend that laws should contain the following:

> the extent of legal liability for the accuracy of the data;
> the extent of rights of privacy over land and property information;
> who owns the copyright to data within the registers;
> who may have access to data;
> who may alter entries in the registers

UNECE, 1996

4.P.3 Public notice

Publicité foncière (F); Edicto de bienes raíces (E)

Public notice defines the process and period by which the administrative system can be legally assumed to have properly informed the public, for example in connection with issues such as adjudication.

A characteristic of the processes of land adjudication and registration, and land consolidation schemes is that they involve the definition and redefinition of rights of owners of the parcel in question, and of other owners of adjacent parcels. A common characteristic of these processes is for there to be a period of public notice of adjudication or consolidation schemes in the area to allow any appeals before they are crystallised into the law. Public notice helps to ensure success of the scheme by encouraging public acceptance and support.

4.R.1 Register
Registre (F); Registro (E)

A register is a facility for recording specified matters.

A register may be a paper based record, kept in loose leaf files or bound into books. It has moved rapidly in the 1990's in sophisticated economies to electronically recorded data, using computer technology. It is becoming increasingly accessible by the internet, for example, for on-line conveyancing.

There may be several registers associated with land and property within one jurisdiction, including for example those related to land taxation and valuation such as the traditional cadastre, and those related to ownership, such as the land register or land book. In some jurisdictions these registers are being integrated with other land information to enable many purposes to be fulfilled.

4.R.2 Registration
Immatriculation (F); Matrícula inmobiliaria / Registro de la propiedad inmueble / Registro esporádico o sistemático (E)

Registration is the process by which rights and interests are recorded in registers. The process of registration in relation to land may follow a range of different options depending not least on the purpose and particular circumstances of the jurisdiction. These may include some at least of land registration, deeds registration, title registration, sporadic registration, systematic registration and registration of transactions.

4.R.3 Registration of transactions
Enregistrement des transactions (F); Registro de transacciones / Registro de instrumentos públicos (E)

Registration of transactions is the process by which transactional changes in rights and interests are recorded in registers.

Registration of transactions is often a legal requirement supporting a registration system. Without such compulsory registration requirements it is often argued that the system would become out of date and thus of progressively reduced value in fulfilling its tasks of maintaining an up to date record of ownership and related land rights. Registration of transactions will usually have a cost associated with it in fees, stamp duty and other transaction costs. In order for a registration system to succeed, whether it is "compulsory" or not, these costs must be sufficiently low to make the registration process viable for the registrant, otherwise alternative markets and unofficial transactions will occur and again undermine the registration system.

4.S.1 Sporadic registration

Sporadic registration of land is the process of registering land on a case-by-case basis usually as the result of a specific trigger such as the sale of the property. When introducing new systems of land registration or land titling it is usual to consider whether the most appropriate approach is for systematic or sporadic registration.

Sporadic registration is usually based on a specific action or actions of the owner of the property to trigger bringing it into the registration system. The most common action used to trigger sporadic registration is the sale of the property. This was, for instance, used as the main trigger for compulsory registration in defined registration areas in England and Wales after 1925.

Sporadic registration has the advantage that it may be less expensive in the short term than systematic registration and that it tends to target most economically active property first. It has the disadvantage that it will take much longer to achieve complete coverage of all titles within the jurisdiction. FIG, 1995

If the intention is to register all (or even most) parcels, then sporadic registration cannot be cheaper, and will likely be more expensive because of lack of economies of scale (e.g., neighbours all having to survey their parcels separately.)

Sporadic registration can also be criticised because the claims of each case are determined separately. Typically, public notice of the claim is a legalistic notice published in a newspaper. The process is not always very transparent. In contrast, systematic registration brings all claims in an area to light at the same time. It allows the population at large to scrutinise the claims being made.

4.S.2 Systematic registration

Systematic registration is the systematic approach to adjudicating, surveying and registering parcels on an area by area basis.

When introducing new systems of land registration or land titling it is usual to consider whether the most appropriate approach is for systematic or sporadic registration.

Systematic registration is relatively expensive in budgetary terms because of the typically large numbers of parcels being dealt with, although on a per parcel basis the average cost per parcel may be significantly lower than with sporadic registration as a result of economies of scale.

Systematic registration has the advantage that it will provide more comprehensive land information within a given time frame. It will also give more people improved rights more quickly, thus supporting the general development impact of increased security of ownership and reduced transaction costs. FIG, 1995

4.T.1 Title deed

Titre foncier (F); Título de tierras / Escritura pública / Título de propiedad (E)

A title is a right of ownership in real property. The title deeds of a property are the documents which evidence or prove ownership of the property.

Under a deeds system of conveyancing, the proof of title is through the demonstration of an unbroken thread of ownership through the sequence of deeds over the requisite number of years.

Under a title registration system, the land certificate may be referred to colloquially as the title deed, although in reality it is a certified copy of an entry in the title register.

4.T.2 Title insurance

Title insurance is an insurance service offered by companies to property purchasers under a deeds based system.

The title insurance underwrites any losses that may result after purchase of the property from discovered defects in the title. The purchaser pays a premium to the insurance company for this service. The service is available both to lenders under a mortgage arrangement, and to property purchasers.

4.T.3 Title registration

Title registration is a system for improving the quality of ownership and proof of title.

There are broadly speaking two parts of the register. The first is a map on which each parcel is demarcated and identified by a unique parcel identifier. The second is a text which records details about the title, the owner and any rights or restrictions associated with the parcel's ownership such as restrictive covenants or mortgages. Under a title registration system a transfer of the property simply results in a change in the name registered. A division of the land or alteration of the boundaries requires amendment to the plan and the issue of new documents or certificates. The official title registration record is definitive. UNECE, 1996

4.T.4 Torrens System

Système Torrens (F); Sistema Torrens (E)

The Torrens System is a system of title registration.

The concept of a "Torrens System" of title registration poses problems as there is no single such system, nor are its characteristics explicitly defined. Even in Australia, the home of the "Torrens System" there is a remarkable diversity of registration systems in the different states. The Torrens System of title registration is named after Sir Robert Torrens who introduced a system of title registration into South Australia in 1858.

The key features of title registration are security, simplicity, accuracy, expedition, cheapness, suitability to its circumstances and completeness of the record.

Three fundamental principles for the success of a title registration system proposed by Ruoff, RUOFF, T., 1957, and generally accepted are:

> The mirror principle – that the register reflects accurately and completely all of the current facts material to the title.
> The curtain principle – that the register is the sole source of information necessary for a purchaser.
> The insurance principle – that anyone who suffers a loss should be compensated.

REFERENCES CHAPTER 4

CARD, R., MURDOCH, J., SCHOFIELD, P., *Law for Estate Management Students*, 4th Ed, Butterworths, London, 1994

HUSSEIN, K., *Conflict between farmers and herders in the semi-arid Sahel and East Africa: A review,* Pastoral Land Tenure Series, No 10, IIED/ODG DEV/University of East Anglia, 1998

LEONARD, R., and LONGBOTTOM, J., *Land Tenure Lexicon: A glossary of terms from English and French speaking West Africa,* International Institute for Environment and Development (IIED), London, 2000

MANTHORPE, J., *UN ECE Land Administration Inventory in Europe, Parts 1 and 2*, HM Land Registry, London, 1997

ROWTON SIMPSON, S., *Land Law and Registration*, Surveyors Publications, London, 1976

RUOFF, T., *An Englishman looks at the Torrens System*, Sydney, 1957

UN, ECONOMIC COMMISSION FOR EUROPE, *Land Administration Guidelines*, UN ECE, Committee on Human Settlements, Geneva, 1996

V. TAX AND ECONOMIC TERMS

IN LAND

CHAPTER 5

Tax and economic terms in land

5.A.1 Annual value

The annual value of land is based on how much the land will rent for on an annual basis.

Property taxation systems used to generate annual taxes are usually based on one of:

> Rental/annual value
> Existing use/capital value
> Highest and best use/capital value
> Unimproved capital value, or
> Artificial bases

The annual value is used in many countries and is based on the rental value as defined in the relevant legislation. This will provide statutorily specified assumptions as to who, landlord or tenant, will be responsible for certain of the running costs in relation to the property.

5.A.2 Arbitration

Arbitraje (E)

Arbitration is the formal process of weighing evidence in order to reach a settlement when the parties are unable to reach agreement on an issue in contention.

Arbitration is a possible solution in situations where two or more parties to a contract are unable to reach agreement. This might occur where a lease contract includes a clause allowing periodic review of the rent to market value. The role of the arbitrator is usually governed by legislation. Arbitrators have certain powers and responsibilities, and deliver decisions based both on the submissions of the parties and on their own expertise in the field.

An arbitrator is distinct from an independent expert. An arbitrator acts in much the same way as a judge, basing the decision only on evidence and arguments submitted to him by the parties. The arbitrator cannot reach a decision without receiving evidence from the parties, or just one of the parties when proceeding *ex parte*. Arbitrators weigh the evidence and arguments on the basis of their expertise. Their award must lie between the two extremes put forward by the parties. RICS, 2002

5.A.3 Assessment

An assessment is usually a term applied to forms of statutory valuation where a value has to be assessed, most commonly related to market value, but where the market will not itself operate to assess value. The most common instances where this is the case are in the assessments of value for property taxes and for compulsory purchase compensation.

In taxation valuations, assessments of the unimproved capital value not only make a similar assumption about a willing buyer and a willing seller, but also assume that none of the improvements to the land have actually been made. In systems of land taxation based on annual value, assumptions are made regarding the relationship between the hypothetical tenant and the hypothetical landlord, and the condition of the property.

In practice assessments are therefore often complex and contentious, with the result that they can generate large bodies of law. In many jurisdictions appeals from assessments will be to a specialist tribunal.

5.A.4 Assessor

Asesor / Tasador (E)

An assessor is a person nominated under a specific piece of legislation to make assessments of value for statutory purposes. These are usually in the context of the preparation of general valuation/assessment rolls for property taxation. An assessor may be a professionally qualified valuer.

5.B.1 Betterment
Valorisation foncière (F); Valorización (E)

"Betterment" is the increase in the value of property as the result of public decisions and intervention. Increases in value may result from, for example:

> Improvements in the utility of property resulting from changes in the use restrictions applying to a property, for example, through the grant of planning permission
> Improvements to the infrastructure increasing accessibility

In some instances the state or the community may be entitled to secure the benefit of any development value by requiring land to pass through public ownership prior to its development into a different use. The statutorily empowered authority in such circumstances is entitled to acquire land that is ripe for development at existing use value, and to sell it to developers for development value. In other cases a part of this increase in value is subject to special taxation.

5.B.2 Betterment levy

Betterment levy is the sum recovered by local authorities from the owners of properties where these properties have been improved by public schemes as contributions to the cost of those schemes.

5.B.3 Building lease

A building lease is a form of lease where the landowner leases land to be developed to a developer.

The building lease will usually be a long term lease, often 99 or 125 years, allowing the developer to amortise the investment in construction and make an appropriate return on the capital invested. The rent paid under the lease may be fixed, or it may be, for example, geared to the head rent paid by the tenant in occupation. The rent under a building lease is usually referred to as a ground rent.

5.C.1 Capital value

The capital value of a property is what a property will sell for.

Property taxation systems used to generate annual taxes are usually based on one of:

- Rental/annual value
- Existing use/capital value
- Highest and best use/capital value
- Unimproved capital value
- Artificial bases

The capital value is used in many countries and is usually based on existing use value, or on the highest and best use value. The relevant basis for valuation will be defined in the relevant legislation under specified assumptions.

5.C.2 Collateral (land)

Nantissement foncier (F)

Property used as collateral is pledged as a guarantee for the repayment of a loan. The most common form of use of collateral is the mortgage.

5.C.3 Commoditisation

Marchandisation (F);
Comercialización de tierras/ Negociaciones inmobiliarias (E)

"Commoditisation" describes the transformation of the land into a commodity that can be bought and sold.

The concept of commoditisation relates to the period of transition from one form of land rights to a market for land. It may thus legitimately be used for the period of transition from a feudal to a market economy, when the basis for access to land changes from feudal service to money. It can be used equally for the change from customary forms of tenure which may preclude in principle the possibility of sale. Access to land in such systems is often in return for fulfilling certain responsibilities to the community or the relevant chief. Commoditisation occurs when such a system moves to one where the land is sold and market relations take the place of customary relations.

A third instance of changing systems is in the transitional economies of the Former Soviet Union, Central and Eastern Europe and elsewhere. Here land is (more or less) moving from a system of state ownership to one of varying degrees of private ownership, with in most cases the intent of introducing normal market economy relationships with the land.

More recently the term commoditisation refers to the rapid innovation of increasingly sophisticated financial vehicles related to real estate. These are driven by the increasing internationalisation of capital and the consequent drive for standardisation. They are also a reaction by the market to try to resolve the perceived disadvantages of real estate as an investment; that it is bulky, costly to purchase, complex expensive to manage and deal with, and illiquid. Examples at the more everyday end of the spectrum include timeshare arrangements. More large scale innovations include single property unit trusts.

5.C.4 Compensation
Indemnización (E)

Compensation is the payment for property taken or adversely affected by another. The payment varies between jurisdictions and may take the form of money, bonds, or exchange with alternative land.

Interference with the rights of ownership of land, whether through compulsory acquisition of those rights or through planning restrictions, may result in a total or partial loss of value of the rights on the part of the owner. In most jurisdictions there are legislative provisions, sometimes enshrined in constitutional guarantees, providing for compensation in respect of such losses. These provisions, the procedures and assumptions that they include, and their relative generosity, vary between jurisdictions.

Examples of the bases of claims for compensation include:
England and Wales: *Claims for compensation for compulsory acquisition where land is taken will include claims for the land taken, for severance and injurious affection to any land retained, and for disturbance. There are also claims for compensation where land is affected by a public scheme, rather than taken. These will be generally*

for different forms of injurious affection. The principle underlying claims for compensation is normally assumed to be that of "equivalence", that the compensation should leave the person no worse off, and no better off than they were prior to the compulsory acquisition.

5.C.5 Condominium

Immeuble en copropriété (F); Propiedad horizontal (E)

Condominium ownership is a form of ownership in which parts of the property are owned individually and parts are owned jointly, as tenants in common. Condominium ownership is particularly common in situations where common ownership of parts of a property is an integral part of the design, as for instance is the case in apartment buildings.

Condominium ownership is distinct from a cooperative, where a corporation holds title to the whole property and individuals have exclusive rights to their units through a lease. It is further distinguished from a planned community where the individual owns the unit and the corporation owns the common parts.

A condominium association has a management committee to ensure that these jointly owned areas are properly maintained, and has powers to raise money from the condominium owners to pay for the costs.

5.C.6 Conflict of interest

A conflict of interest is a situation where an individual or corporate entity is invited to act on behalf of one party, but has an actual or potential relationship with or interest in the other party or parties.

Professional associations dealing with real estate generally include a statement of ethical practice which incorporates standards relating to conflicts of interest. These bind the membership to stated standards of practice and reassure clients of the standards of ethics that they can expect. FIG, 1998

5.D.1 Depreciated replacement cost

The depreciated replacement cost of a property is the value of the site in its existing use plus the gross replacement cost of the buildings after appropriate allowance has been made for depreciation.

The technical definition of valuation terms is increasingly the subject of national and international valuation standards and these are available from the International Valuation Standards Committee. IVSC, 2001.

5.D.2 Development

Land development is the application of resources to improve land that should enable it to be used more efficiently.

5.D.3 Development value

Development value is the value of a property under given assumptions about permitted development. A property with development potential is likely therefore to have a different existing use value to its development value.

5.D.4 Dilapidations

Dilapidations are the claim by a landlord for compensation for the failure of a tenant to maintain and repair a property under the terms of a lease.

Dilapidations arise at the end of a lease and result from the tenant's liabilities for maintenance and repair. The extent of any claim will therefore depend on the facts of what the tenant has been responsible for under the lease, and how well these obligations have been fulfilled. The usual practice is for a schedule of dilapidations to be drawn up by or on behalf of the landlord and for this to be served on the tenant prior to the expiry of the lease or tenancy. The tenant may, of course, contest this claim. Once agreed, the tenant may either undertake the identified works or reach an appropriate cash settlement with the landlord. FAO, 2001

Examples of dilapidations claimable under an agricultural tenancy include:
England and Wales: *Under an Agricultural Holdings Act tenancy, a landlord will be able to claim dilapidations from the tenant, where appropriate, on the termination of the tenancy. The heads of claim may include claims for:*

> *foul land and pasture infested with perennial weeds;*
> *maintenance of fences, hedges and gates;*
> *maintenance of ditches and drains;*
> *repairs to buildings and fixed equipment;*
> *cross-cropping of the land out of rotation; and*
> *selling off of produce in the last year of the tenancy.*

5.D.5 Disturbance

Disturbance is a head of claim for compensation for losses resulting from the taking of land, other than the taking of the land itself, or the associated effects of the taking on land retained.

Disturbance claims may form a part of claims for compensation where a person vacates land as a result of being expropriated and dispossessed. This is likely to include in many jurisdictions a measure of additional compensation for loss of a home, and for loss of goodwill where businesses are forced to move. Disturbance is an accepted element of a compensation claim in many countries.

5.D.6 Duty of care

The duty of care defines the responsibilities of people to one another, and is particularly important for agents, valuers, landowners and those responsible for land and buildings.

The concept of a duty of care is a central part of the English common law concept of negligence. It is an important extension of the law as it identifies responsibilities of people to one another in specific cases, and has regard to standards of a defendant's conduct; with the general requirement that such conduct should be that of the "reasonable person". Although it is an area of continual development in the courts, in principle a duty of care will be recognised when:

> it is foreseeable by the defendant that negligence on his part will cause injury, damage or loss;
> there is a relationship of sufficient closeness between the parties; and,
> that it is just and reasonable to impose liability.

CARD, R., MURDOCH, J., SCHOFIELD, P., 1994

5.E.1 Environment

Environnement (F); Medio ambiente (E)

Environment is defined as: "The combined external conditions affecting life, development and survival of an organism or an ecosystem." CHOUDHURY, K., and JANSEN, L. J. M., 1999

5.E.2 Estate management

Estate management is a term most frequently used in the United Kingdom. It is broadly included within land management. The estate manager undertakes management of urban and rural real estate, whether as an owner or adviser, and whether in the public or the private sector. He or she deals, therefore, with issues relating to:

> the achievement of an acceptable return from the land interests owned.
> the maintenance or enhancement of the value of the land interests owned.
> such returns and values are likely to include a mixture of financial/economic, social and environmental (including sustainability) qualities.

NIX, J., HILL, P., WILLIAMS, N., and BAUGH, J., 1998

5.E.3 Existing use value

The existing use value is the best price that a property can be sold for assuming its current use will continue. The technical definition of valuation terms is increasingly the subject of national and international valuation standards and these are available from the International Valuation Standards Committee. IVSC, 2001.

5.F.1 Fixtures

Accesorios (E)

Fixtures are things that have become part of the land in English legal terms by virtue of their attachment to the land.

Whether they are to be considered as fixtures or chattels depends upon the degree of annexation and the purpose of annexation. So, for example, cinema seats have been held to be fixtures and a part of the land, whereas tapestries fixed to a wall have been considered chattels. The distinction is significant because fixtures at the time of a mortgage are included in that mortgage, and at the time of the contract for sale are included in the conveyance, unless specifically excluded.

5.G.1 Ground rent

The ground rent is a rent payable to the landlord of a building lease.

Ground rent is also used as a general term for any long term rental that is significantly below full rental value created by the sale of a lease at a premium.

5.G.2 Guarantee

Caution (F); Caución / Fianza / Garantía / Aseguramiento (E)

A guarantee is an assurance provided by an individual or other entity that something, often a contract, will be fulfilled.

A guarantor may provide a guarantee that a person or company will fulfil a contract, and will thus frequently be included as a party to the contract.

5.H.1 Headlessee

A lease or tenancy of land is a contract entered into between a lessor or landlord, who leases the land to the lessee or tenant. It is possible in some cases for the lessee or tenant to sublease the property to one or more parties. In such a case the direct tenant of the landlord is the headlessee, and the tenants of the headlessee are subtenants.

5.I.1 Independent expert

An independent expert is a specialist appointed to decide a settlement when the parties are unable to reach agreement on an issue in contention.

Appointing an independent expert may be one solution in situations where two or more parties to a contract are unable to reach agreement, for example, where a lease contract includes a clause allowing periodic review of the rent to market value. The role of the independent expert is not governed by legislation. Independent experts decide on the basis of their own knowledge and experience, but may also receive evidence and, where agreed, submissions from the parties.

An independent expert is distinct from an arbitrator. An independent expert, in the context of a valuation dispute, acts as a valuer, with the duty to discover the facts and decide accordingly. Any submissions of the parties do not limit this award. There are no procedures laid down in legislation and enforcement of an award would have to be based on a separate action. An independent expert has liability for any negligence. RICS, 2002

5.I.2 Inheritance tax / Death duties

Inheritance tax or death duties are taxes on assets on the death of an owner, some jurisdictions generalise this as a tax on the transfer of assets.

Land and buildings will usually be subject to such taxes, although there may be exemptions for transfers between spouses, and in some jurisdictions there may be reduced rates of tax according to the closeness of the family relationship of the beneficiary. There may also be specific relief for certain types of asset, particularly for family owned businesses and farms.

5.I.3 Injurious affection

Injurious affection is the "… loss sustained to that part remaining, by the carrying out of some activity on the land which has been acquired." WIDDICOMBE, D., and MOORE, V., 1975

5.L.1 Land capital

Capital foncier (F); Capital de tierras (E)

Land is viewed in economic terms as a factor of production. Land, as defined, including the land itself, buildings, plantations and other improvements, also has a capital value as an asset. This asset value has many uses, ranging for example, from security for mortgage loans to use as a tax base.

5.L.2 Land economy

Land economy has been defined as 'the study of the management of resources of people and land and is concerned with the economic, legal and sociological factors which affect the ownership of land both at the private, local and national levels. In short it concerns the relationship of human society to the land through the institution of property …' ACQUAYE, E., 1980

5.L.3 Land loan

Prêt foncier (F)

Loans of land are distinct from a lease or tenancy of land, as there is normally no rent payable for the use of the land, although payments may be made as a sign of recognition of the loan by the borrower.

Land loans are common in West Africa with borrowing usually by recent arrivals in a village or by younger members of a family. Usually the village authorities or individuals will show the land to the potential borrower and arrangements will be made orally in front of witnesses. These would include those primarily involved and possibly other members of the community. Loans may be long or short term, and may in fact go on for generations. Where land is becoming more scarce, owners of land are less happy to lend good quality fields for more than a season because the statutory law in some countries may allow the user to appropriate the property rights in due course. VIERICH. H., and DRABO, M. G., 1987.

*In **Burkina Faso** land loans are an important part of flexibility in land use which enables sustainable land use practices to cater for such eventualities as immigration, illness and changes in the family. In practice it is very difficult for someone to refuse to lend land if they have land available, unless the proposed borrower is demonstrably a bad character. LEONARD, R., and LONGBOTTOM, J., 2000*

5.L.4 Land market
Marché foncier (F)

The land market is where buyers and sellers of interests in land meet.

Land and buildings typically comprise 50% to 75% of a country's national wealth. The percentage varies according to the characteristics of the national economy. Countries with a lower degree of economic development and consequently fewer alternative investments, as is the case in most transitional and developing economies, could be expected to have a higher percentage of national wealth in land and buildings.

Land and the land market are critically important in economic development. Economically efficient use of real property results from:

> sound legal frameworks in relevant areas
> efficient markets promoted through confidence resulting from transparent market mechanisms, and the availability of specialist knowledge and advice
> positive management of the real property resource

Leaving market forces to determine the ownership, user and, usually subject to planning and environmental considerations, the use of land and buildings allows the price mechanism of the market to move the economic resource of land and buildings towards its highest and economically most efficient use. It is important to recognise that the functioning of the market must be transparent, soundly administered, diverse and flexible to achieve this end, conditions that are often not adequately achieved.

Actors in the market are usually only active infrequently during their lifetimes. Land transactions are, however, often the largest single transactions made by an individual and require specialist knowledge. It is therefore common practice for the vendor, and perhaps the purchaser, to use specialist advisers to assist in the transaction.

5.L.5 Land rent

Rente foncière (F); Renta / Renta de bines raíces / Renta de la tierra / Renat real / Renta del suelo (E)

In practical terms rent is the payment for the hire of land and buildings and is a function of the supply and demand for that particular type of property in that particular location.

Factors affecting the rental of land or buildings vary according to their use. With agricultural land, for example, the following characteristics are among those likely to be significant: location, access to services and communications, soil quality, drainage, aspect, slope, improvements on the land including buildings, etc.
There are many rent related terms in current use, including:

> rack rent (full market rental value)
> rent passing (the rent payable under a lease)
> ground rent (the rent payable under a ground lease)
> peppercorn rent (a nominal rent payable under a ground lease)

5.L.6 Land speculation

Spéculation foncière (F);
Especulación de tierras / Especulación de bienes raíces (E)

Land speculation is the purchase of land with the intention of selling it, generally quickly, at a substantial profit.
Speculation in most commodities, but particularly in land, is typically thought to be undesirable, based on the argument that it increases the cost of the resource to those who will actually use it. There have, as a result, been efforts in several jurisdictions to reduce the return to

speculators, usually following periods of rapid increase in land prices. An example of such an approach is the Land Sales Act, 1974, in Fiji, where a law was introduced to regulate speculative and other dealings in land and taxation on the profits thereon.

Alternative views would be that, unless there is a real capacity to control supply of land, a purchaser in a speculative situation is making a risky investment, and accordingly can expect a commensurate return in the event of it proving successful

5.L.7 Lease-back

Cession-bail (F); Cesión de arrendamiento / Transpaso (E)

A sale and lease-back is where an owner-occupier agrees to sell the freehold or equivalent to an investment owner. The investment owner agrees to enter simultaneously into a lease with the existing owner-occupier who then becomes the tenant of the investment owner.

Leasebacks generally take place because the owner wishes to raise capital, and it is a relatively cheap way of doing so particularly when interest rates are high. It is commonly used with commercial property and in development property in the UK, and has even been a feature of the agricultural land market during periods when agricultural land was an attractive investment.

5.L.7 Lien

Embargo preventivo / Derecho de retención (E)

A lien is a charge placed over an asset that is used as a security for a loan. It is common practice for example for banks to take out a lien over a farmer's crops or other specified assets as security for a loan, thus reducing their risk and enabling them to charge lower rates of interest. Liens are often registered at a statutorily enabled agency.

A lien is also a charge on property for the payment of a debt not associated with a loan secured against the property. Some jurisdictions file a tax lien against the property owner and property if property taxes are not paid. The owner cannot sell or refinance the property without first paying off the lien.

5.M.1 Mass appraisal

Mass appraisal is the process of valuing a large number of properties at the same time using standardized procedures.

Computer assisted mass appraisal (CAMA) refers to the automation of the process. The approaches to large-scale valuations are well suited to the application of computerised techniques. They are particularly associated with the use of computers to analyse markets using multiple regression techniques, and with the application of this data in the valuation process. FAO 2002.

5.M.2 Mortgage

Garantie foncière (F); Hipoteca (E)

A mortgage of land is a transfer of an interest in the land as security for a debt.

The mortgagee (creditor) can use the mortgaged land to settle the debt in the event of the mortgagor (debtor) not being willing or able to repay the debt. The most common approach to this is by the sale of the land, with the creditor taking the debt, including costs, etc, out of the proceeds of the sale. Mortgages form a very important part of an economy, and particularly so of developed market economies.

5.M.3 Mortgage bank

Crédit immobilier (F); Crédito inmobiliario (E)

A mortgage bank is a bank that specialises in granting credits for the purchase of property where the credit is secured against the real estate by a mortgage. Credit is generally granted by the lender in return for the borrower undertaking to repay the loaned capital, in addition to interest incurred, over the life of the loan.

The amount of interest charged reflects the risk of the lender defaulting on payments, and the specific market conditions in which the lending takes place. The common approach used by mortgage banks to reduce the risk, and hence the rate of interest payable, is for the lender to take some security for the loan, often as a lien or a mortgage.

5.O.1 Open market value

The open market value is the best price that a property can be sold for.

The technical definition of valuation terms is increasingly the subject of national and international valuation standards and these are available from the International Valuation Standards Committee. IVSC, 2001.

5.P.1 Premium

A premium is a capital sum paid at the outset of a lease in consideration of a reduction in the property's rental.

5.P.2 Professional indemnity insurance

Professional indemnity insurance is insurance that will cover losses sustained by clients as a result of negligent advice.

Professional institutions representing professional advisers, such as surveyors or valuers, usually require their members to accept responsibility to their clients for their advice. This position of a duty of care is supported through the law of negligence.

5.P.3 Profit rent

A profit rent arises where tenants pay less to their landlord than the rent they receive from their subtenant.

Where there is no subtenant, the profit rent is the difference between the rent paid to the landlord and the market rental value or rack rent. If there is no such difference there is no profit rent.

5.R.1 Rack rent

The rack rent of a property is its full market rental value.

5.R.2 Rating

Rating is a term commonly used in the United Kingdom and in countries influenced by English Common Law to refer to raising of an annual property tax based on market related value. Originally the term referred to taxes based on the annual value of the property, but it is now quite common for the term to be used generally whether the tax is based on annual or capital value.

5.R.3 Real estate
Immeuble / Immobilier (F); Inmueble / Inmobiliario (E)

Real estate is distinct from personal property. It is the same as land in the English Common Law understanding.

5.S.1 Security / Guarantee
Gage (F); Prenda / Prenda agraria / Pignoración (E)

A security is an asset that is used to secure a loan.
A security may be either a real estate asset, in which case the security is generally referred to as a mortgage, or personal property such as agricultural products where the security would generally be in the form of a lien. It may also be used in the context of loans to government which are often referred to as government bonds, stocks, or securities. In the event of the debtor defaulting on the loan, where it is secured by a mortgage or a lien, the creditor has the right to sell the asset and to satisfy the debt out of the sum realised.

5.S.2 Severance.

Severance is the "... loss sustained from the acquisition of part only of an owner's land, where the value of the part remaining with him is reduced disproportionately to the value of the whole."
WIDDICOMBE, D., and MOORE, V., 1975

Examples of severance include where a dairy farm loses a significant part of its acreage. The remaining land may be inadequate to support a dairy enterprise, thus reducing disproportionately the value of the land retained.

5.S.3 Site value

The site value is a form of unimproved capital value.
Site value is sometimes used as the basis for a property tax.

5.S.4 Stamp duty

Stamp duty is a tax on the transfer of property.

The tax is called stamp duty as it is based on the stamping of the document executing the transfer. Stamp duty regimes vary according to the jurisdiction. Stamp duty is usually based on the value of the property in question, although this value is, in some cases, set at official prices which are often significantly different from market values.

5.S.5 Standards of measurement

Standard bases of measurement are important to ensure uniformity and accuracy. Standards are legislated in some jurisdictions and dealt with by codes of practice in others. The UK based professional institution dealing with property related matters, The Royal Institution of Chartered Surveyors, publishes the Code of Measuring Practice. The Code provides core definitions and examples for the measurement of different types of buildings and land parcels for various purposes. RICS, 2001.

5.T.1 Tax base

Base d'imposition (F);
Base gravable / Gravamen / Impuesto predial (E)

The tax base is the value basis on which a property tax is levied.
There are several different approaches in use around the world. The most common approaches used are based on:

> capital values, with improvements, whether existing use value, or highest and best use (open market) value
> rental (annual) values, on the basis of existing use
> capital values, unimproved, whether existing use value, or highest and best use (open market) value

There are also instances where just the value of the improvements are used as the basis, usually on a depreciated replacement cost of the buildings basis as in Ghana, or where an artificial or non-market value base is used. These last include taxes based on a per square metre basis for buildings, and a per hectare basis for land. FAO, 2002.

5.U.1 Unimproved capital value

The unimproved capital value of land is a statutorily defined tax value based on the price of the land without any buildings or other improvements.

Property taxation systems used to generate annual taxes are usually based on one of:

- Rental/annual value
- Existing use/capital value
- Highest and best use/capital value
- Unimproved capital value
- Artificial bases

The unimproved capital value of a property is used in several jurisdictions as the basis for annual taxation. It has virtually no uses other than for taxation and is an artificial value that has no direct market quotient, although it is market value based. The concept of using the unimproved capital value was developed in the writings of Henry George, a 19th century American economist who advocated that all tax should be based on a single property tax based on the value of the land less improvements.

Although the unimproved capital value is defined differently in different jurisdictions, the definitions revolve around a common core that the land is assumed to be in its natural condition, but that it has the benefit of all of the real world infrastructural and locational advantages enjoyed by the land. These include roads, railways, public services and amenities, the potential use, and any other attributes not due to improvements on the property.

The unimproved capital value is used fairly widely, for example, in Australia, New Zealand and the Pacific region.

5.V.1 Valuation standards

Standard bases of valuation are important to ensure uniformity and accuracy. Standards are legislated in some jurisdictions and dealt with by codes of practice in others.

The development and adoption of valuation standards is increasingly seen as a critical issue for economic development, in a similar way to accounting standards. The development of appropriate standards in both fields follows a similar pattern, with an overall international committee, regional groupings often to prepare regional equivalents and stimulate professional and practice development, and national committees producing national standards tailored to the individual country's circumstances.

5.V.2 Valuer

A valuer is someone qualified to undertake a valuation.

The question of whether the state should regulate real estate appraisal or valuation activity is answered differently in different jurisdictions around the world. Some have statutory regulation and licensing regimes, for example, various states in Australia, Fiji, and Malaysia. Others, such as the UK leave regulation and licensing/qualification to self-regulating professional associations.

5.W.1 Willing seller

A willing seller is one who is "neither eager nor reluctant to sell."

Definitions of market value include the assumption that there is a willing seller. This term is generally the subject of further explanation in the commentaries attaching to the valuation standards. The assumption of a willing seller is critical to defining open market value. This is because the vendor should be taken as a hypothetical owner who is "neither eager nor reluctant" to sell. The real owner's actual situation is irrelevant in this assessment.

5.Y.1 Years' purchase

The years' purchase is the present value of the right to receive an annual income.

The years' purchase comprises a formula for use in property valuations which discounts the value of future income by an appropriate yield or interest rate. This interest rate reflects the market's perception of the risk attaching to the income.

REFERENCES CHAPTER 5

ACQUAYE, E., *Education for the Land Economy Profession in Developing Countries*, The Role of the CASLE (Commonwealth Association of Surveying and Land Economy) Professions in Rural Development Programmes in the South Pacific, Conference Proceedings, CASLE, Papua New Guinea, 1980

CARD, R., MURDOCH, J., SCHOFIELD, P., *Law for Estate Management Students*, 4th Ed, Butterworths, London, 1994

CHOUDHURY, K., and JANSEN, L. J. M., Eds.,*Terminology for Integrated Resources Management and Planning*, FAO/UNEP, Rome, 1999

FAO, *Good Practice Guidelines for Agricultural Leasing Arrangements.* FAO Land Tenure Studies No. 2. Rome. 2001

FAO, *Rural property tax systems in Central and Eastern Europe.* FAO Land Tenure Studies No. 5. Rome 2002

IVSC, *International Valuation Standards*, International Valuation Standards Committee, London, 2001

FIG, *Constituting Professional Associations*, International Federation of Surveyors, FIG publication number 16, Copenhagen, 1998

NIX, J., HILL, P., WILLIAMS, N., and BAUGH, J., *Land and Estate Management*, Packard Publishing, Chichester, UK, 1998

RICS, *Guidance Notes for Surveyors Acting as Arbitrators or as Independent Experts in Rent Reviews*. Royal Institution of Chartered Surveyors, London, 2002

RICS, *Code of Measuring Practice*. Royal Institution of Chartered Surveyors, London, 2001

VIERICH. H., and DRABO, M. G., *ICRISAT village reports: Land use and tenure*, International Crops Research Institute for the Semi-Arid Tropics, Patancheru, India, 1987

WIDDICOMBE, D., and MOORE, V., *A General Survey of English Law*, in GARNER, J. F., Ed., *Compensation for Compulsory Purchase : A Comparative Study*, UK National Committee of Comparative Law, London, 1975

VI. NON-STATE SYSTEMS OF LAND ADMINISTRATION

CHAPTER 6

Non-state systems of land administration

6.C.1 Chief (land/lineage)

Chef de terre ou responsable de la terre (F);
Autoridades locales tradicionales/ Jefe / aldea /
Autoridades político-administrativas (E)

The land chief is a descendant of the first occupier of an area who acts as the mediator between man and land and who traditionally holds power over land in customary societies without actually owning it.

The land chief has both quasi-political and quasi-religious or spiritual roles in relation to land. He is the highest authority on land issues and the chief of his lineage, but there may be other chiefs responsible for matters of war, religion and dispute settlement, for example.

The powers of the land chief may include:

- Division of land between the clans in the lineage group
- Permitting settlers access to land
- Arbitration of disputes relating to land
- Guarantee of the group's boundaries

The allocational powers of the land chief tend to decline as pressure on the land increases because of population growth. Once parcels reach a practically irreducible size, customary succession rules determine how land passes between generations, and the land chief's role is reduced to resolving disputes and to ceremonial functions.

6.C.2 Custom / Customary

Coutumes / Coutumier (F);
Costumbres / Consuetudinario (E)

A custom is an action or practice that has taken place since time immemorial that is not regulated by the state or other authority outside the social group, and which is reinforced by customary usage.

Local custom may also be recognised in the formal legal systems of the world, for example, local custom is recognised by English law where it has been continuously enjoyed since "time immemorial", where it is certain and not unreasonable, and where it is compulsory. Demonstrating time immemorial in this context technically requires proof that the custom existed in 1189. In practice, this will be presumed if the practice could have taken place in 1189, and the oldest local inhabitant affirms its historic existence.

6.C.3 Customary land law / rights

Droit foncier coutumier (F);
Derechos tradicionales o consuetudinarios de tierra (E)

Customary land law regulates rights to enjoy some use of land that arises through customary, unwritten practice rather than through written or codifed law.

6.F.1 Fishery rights

Fishery rights are rights existing in freshwater and marine fisheries which enable the holder to have access for fishing purposes. Water and fishery rights vary considerably from place to place.

*In **West Africa** traditional management of inland fisheries was based on control of water. These rights, as with land rights, were granted to the first occupiers by the spirits of the water, and were in turn managed by the chiefs of the water. The water chief's functions include arranging the fishing calendar in the light of spawning seasons, regulating fishing practices and access and arbitrating in disputes. In many West African countries water rights have been nationalised and regulation and access are now controlled by the state. LEONARD, R., and LONGBOTTOM, J., 2000*

*The indigenous population in **Fiji** enjoys fishery rights both inland and in the marine reef areas that have been demarcated by the Native Fisheries Commission. These fishery rights are held in defined areas by the designated clan group, whose members are recorded in the Vola ni Kawa Bula that is maintained by the Native Land Commission.*

*In **New Zealand**, the Waitangi Tribunal has considered the traditional fishery claims of the indigenous Maori people and has ruled that they should benefit from the quota fees paid for marine fishing.*

6.I.1 Indigenous
Indigène (F); Indígena (E)

Indigenous signifies someone who is intimately connected with the land where he lives, who has not arrived by immigration or is not in passage. The idea "indigenous" is necessarily relative. It often expresses a cultural or property claim.

6.L.1 Lineage
Lignage (F); Linaje (E)

A lineage is a group which has common lines of ancestry, whether these are patrilineal or matrilineal.

The head of the ancestral group commonly governs access to the lineage land as the land chief. The members of the lineage can trace themselves back linearly to a common ancestor.

6.L.2 Lineage land
Espace lignager (F)

Lineage land is land available for the use of the members of the lineage.

*On the floodplain of the **Mauritanian bank of the Senegal River** where the land is flooded annually, the Toucouleur land system is a good example of lineage land and its management.*

The land does not belong to an individual. It belongs to extended social groups, lineages or collectives. Within these social groups the lands are divided between the families that will cultivate them. The lands are managed by the head of the lineage who distributes the parcels to each of the adult males in the lineage. This allocation lasts until a marriage or a death stimulates a redistribution.

The lineage land stays undivided. Moreover it is inalienable whether to members of the lineage or to third parties. The individual and the head of the lineage himself does not have the right to alienate the land to an outsider. It is the collective lineage group that is the owner, not the head of the lineage. On the death of the head of the lineage, the lineage land is inherited collectively by the lineage and the management passes to the next chief in succession.
LEONARD, R., and LONGBOTTOM, J., 2000

6.M.1 Matrilineal
Matrilignage (F); Matrilinaje (E)

A matrilineal lineage group is one where the line of descent and membership is transmitted by the female.

To illustrate how a matrilineal group works, for two individuals to appear in the same parental group, they must trace their descent down the female line. A man and the son of his brother for example would not appear in the same group. The son of the brother would be a part of his mother's group.

Although matrilineal lineage determines the constituent members of a group and its inheritance practices, it does not necessarily mean that property will be held by women in such systems. Females in matrilineal societies do, however, tend to have better access to land than in patrilineal societies. LEONARD, R., and LONGBOTTOM, J., 2000

6.N.1 Non-indigenous
Allochtone (F); Foráneo / Extranjero / Exótico (E)

Non-indigenous refers to an entity or concept that originally comes from outside the area specified.

Non-indigenous may commonly refer to people, but may also include for example laws and customs. Non-indigenous people, whether viewed simply as "immigrants" to an area or as people from outside who are from a specific ethnic background, may find it difficult to integrate with the indigenous people and their customs. They may experience particular problems over access to land.

6.P.1 Pasture master
Maître des pâturages (F)

The pasture master is responsible for managing the pasture lands of a lineage group.

The pasture lands are possessed by one or more family from the same lineage group. The pasture master has absolute control over the grazing but not over the land which is held patrimonially. The appointment of the pasture master is on the advice of the lineage group as it is not an hereditary function.

6.P.2 Patrilineal
Patrilignage (F); Patrilinaje (E)

A patrilineal lineage group is one where the line of descent and membership is transmitted by the male. The large majority of traditional societies in Africa are patrilineal.
LEONARD, R., and LONGBOTTOM, J., 2000

6.P.3 Priest of the land
Prêtre de la terre (F)

The priest of the land is responsible for limited functions in relation to land, including setting out the calendar of works on the land. The priest of the land only exercises limited functions in the area of land relations.

The chief of the land has a social and cultural role that can extend to include those of the priest of the land. These may include looking after the sequence of works and their intervals or putting right any action that puts the life of the community in danger. The chief of the land can therefore exercise the functions of the priest of the land in certain circumstances, but the reverse is not possible. ROULAND, N., 1988

In practice the two positions are quite close. They depend to a great extent on the history of the village and on the sharing out of responsibilities between lineages of more or less equal power.

6.R.1 Right of clearance / Axe rights

Droit de la hache (F)

Rights of clearance arise from the clearing or cutting of bush with the agreement of the first occupier and thereafter are based on continuous usage.

The right of clearance is closely associated with the right of fire. These signify that the person who cuts or burns the natural vegetation has the right to cultivate the cleared land.

6.R.2 Right of first occupancy

Droit du premier occupant (F);
Derecho del primer ocupante (E)

The right of first occupancy is the indissoluble link between the first occupier, the group and the land.

The ritual following the first occupation of land linked the spiritual and terrestrial powers on that land and formed the basis for the indissoluble link between the first occupier, his ancestral group and the land. The present senior descendant of the first occupier assumes the role of chief (land/lineage) and mediates between the spiritual and terrestrial.

Under customary practices this right refers to:

> The first clearer of the land, the ancestral founder of the lineage group to which the land is inalienably attached

> The right of fire and the right of clearance

The two last mentioned rights can also create a right of use on uncultivated land with the agreement of the authority that possesses a prior right on the land. This right returns to the antecedent lineage when cultivation finishes.

The right of first occupation poses the problem of knowing the effective ownership of these lands in the context of modern legislation. The development of value and alienability of the land in rural areas endangers the use rights acquired by non-indigenous people from the lineage groups of the chiefs of the land/lineage. VERDIER, R., 1986

IMAGE 6

6.R.1 Right of clearance / Axe rights

Land clearance in a hilly district of Japan.

M. Griffin, FAO photo.

6.S.1 Sacred wood

Bois sacré (F); Bosque sagrado (E)

A sacred wood is a wood which has a spiritual significance where the land is held by the local spirits and its spiritual character is venerated.

The legal recognition of sacred land and its inviolability creates problems for agricultural extension on the sacred woodland conserved by the village.

6.S.2 System of succession

Système de succession (F); Sistema de sucesión (E)

A system of succession is an approach to passing land. A distinction is drawn between succession by horizontal transmission (brother to brother), by vertical succession (father to oldest son), or equal succession (to all children).

6.V.1 Village headman

Chef de village (F); Autoridades locales tradicionales / Jefe / Aldea / Autoridades político-administrativas (E)

The village headman, who may also be a customary chief, is usually the administrative head of the village who derives his authority from the state, or from customary law. In some countries, there may be a hierarchy of paramount chief / chief / village headman / family head / individual household.

There is a distinction in many societies between the customary and the administrative hierarchies.

> *The customary chief has the ultimate political responsibility in the village community, in which he may or may not be assisted by one or more chiefs of the land. In some cases village chiefs carry out the function of chiefs of the land.*
>
> *This duality of chieftainship results from the system of alliance between ethnic groups or from the presence of new arrivals.*
> ROULAND, N., 1988

The customary village chief is also the administrative chief when he is recognised as the representative of the state. More frequently, two chiefs represent, respectively, the customary authority and the administrative authority in the village.

This dual authority relating to the land, arising from the two different sources of legitimacy, increases the feeling of insecurity when there are land disputes. At the same time, informal practices develop, leading to negotiated solutions on a case by case basis. MATHIEU, P., 1990

*The village headman (turaga ni koro) in **Fiji** is appointed by the central Fijian administration to carry out their administrative functions. The appointment is not a popular one, and would not normally be carried out by the customary chief. It would be considered below the dignity of the customary chief to be the servant of the government to his own people. The village headman is responsible for organising village cleaning, house building and carrying out the orders of the district administrator.*
NAYACAKALOU, R., 1978

6.W.1 Water management

Maîtrise de l'eau (F); Dominio sobre el agua / Fontanero / Aguatero (E)

Water management includes the management of both fresh and marine water for fisheries and other purposes.

Water and fishery rights vary considerably from place to place

Water management includes management of fishery rights under customary practices. The chief of the water specialises in water management. The chief of the water has specific powers to exercise exclusive control over a given fishery that he has inherited or that is part of the property of the lineage. Each village may have several chiefs of the water according to how many lineage fisheries there are to manage. On the other hand, some sections of the river bank are often managed by a single chief of the water from the village.
BARRIERE, O., AND C., 1997

IMAGE 7

6.W.1 Water management

Hydrology technician explaining the use of a motor pump to supply additional irrigation to farmers in Cambodia.

FAO photo.

Water management includes the technical management of irrigated land. The control of water results from investment in development, but its effectiveness depends on good collective discipline for the use of the water and, in the medium to long term, on good maintenance of the irrigation network. Exerting this discipline, and undertaking the maintenance effectively, depend on institutional and organisational factors which are linked to the social relationships between the farmers.

The increased value of irrigated lands is an important asset for the rural population, particularly for non-peasant farmers who have invested capital from other, usually urban, sources in improving the land.
MATHIEU, P., 1990

REFERENCES CHAPTER 6

BARRIERE, O., and C., *Approches environnementales : systèmes fonciers dans le delta intérieur du Niger: de l'implosion du droit traditionnel à la recherche d'un droit propice à la sécurisation foncière*, in LE ROY, E., KARSENTY, A., and BERTRAND, A., *La sécurisation foncière en Afrique : pour une gestion viable des ressources renouvelables*, Karthala, Paris, 1996

LEONARD, R., and LONGBOTTOM, J., *Land Tenure Lexicon: A glossary of terms from English and French speaking West Africa,* International Institute for Environment and Development (IIED), London, 2000

MATHIEU, P., *Usages de la loi et pratiques foncières dans les aménagements irrigués*, in *Politique Africaine*, No 40, 1990

NAYACAKALOU, R., *Tradition and change in the Fijian village*, South Pacific Social Sciences Association, Institute of Pacific Studies, University of the South Pacific, Fiji, 1978

ROULAND, N., *Anthropologie juridique*, PUF, Droit politique et théorique, 1988

VERDIER, R., *Civilisations paysannes et traditions juridiques*, in *Systèmes fonciers à la ville et au village*, Paris, L'Harmattan, 1986

VII. LAND IN AN AGRICULTURAL, PASTORAL AND FORESTRY CONTEXT

CHAPTER 7

Land in an agricultural, pastoral and forestry context

7.A.1 Agrarian systems / structures

Systèmes et structures agraires (F)

An agrarian system, after Mazoyer, is a (predominantly agricultural) way of exploiting an environment that has been established over a period of time and is durable, is adapted to the bio-climatic conditions of the given area and is responsive to the conditions and to the social needs of the time.

The expression agrarian system looks at the interaction between bio-ecological, socio-economic, cultural and political systems, across agricultural practices.

7.A.2 Agriculture

Agriculture (F); Agricultura (E)

A narrow definition of agriculture includes cultivation of crops and animal husbandry as well as forestry, fisheries, and the development of land and water resources.

A broader definition of agriculture includes in addition agro-industries, manufacturing of agricultural inputs and machinery, regional and river development, and rural development.

7.A.3 Agroforestry

Agroforesterie (F); Agroforestería (E)

Agroforestry is a collective name for land use systems and technologies where woody perennials (trees, shrubs, palms, bamboos, etc) are deliberately used on the same land management unit as agricultural crops and/or animals, in some form of spatial arrangement or temporal sequence." In agroforestry systems there are both ecological and economic interactions between the different components. CHOUDHURY, K., and JANSEN, L. J. M., 1999

IMAGE 8

7.A.3 Agroforestry

Agroforestry in practice in Zimbabwe.
Food crops can be intercropped with trees.

G. Diana, FAO photo.

There are two basic agroforestry systems: simultaneous and sequential. Simultaneous systems have trees and crops or animals growing together on the same piece of land, while in sequential systems crops and trees take turns in occupying most of the same space, minimising their competition.

7.A.4 Agropastoralism
Agropastoralisme (F); Agropastoril (E)

Agropastoralism is a mode of production that combines field culture and husbandry with the use of pasture areas.

7.A.5 Allodial
Alleu (F)

Allodial rights are absolute rights of ownership in land that do not have any feudal superior. Full private ownership, the absolute right of ownership, is subject only to the state's right of eminent domain.

The English law freehold, or fee simple, is not allodial as it technically remains subject to the Crown's feudal superiority. Allodial rights exist in other jurisdictions which have an English Common Law foundation, including the USA and Ghana.

7.A.6 Animal husbandry / Cattle breeding / Ranching

Husbandry is usually defined in the context of farming as livestock or animal husbandry, however, in practice this a little restrictive. Husbandry's definition in a farming context may also include other forms of husbandry including of the field and vine, besides animals.
Husbandry in broad terms includes the general productive process in economic endeavour. In farming, animal husbandry can be looked at in three broad categories which take into account a combination of four different characteristics:

> the way of life
> the characteristics of the natural resources (water, pasture), whether permanent or seasonal, and according to the levels of production

> the relations with other agricultural activities
> the types of movement made

On the basis of these can be distinguished nomadic, transhumant and sedentary husbandry.

Nomadic husbandry is a form of husbandry where the husbandry with the way of life of the groups that practice it are fundamentally intermixed. Nomadic husbandry does not have any complimentarity or association with working on the land. It is the principal activity of a group or tribe, organised in part on the basis of access to water resources. There is also a "pure" system of nomadic husbandry based on movements after the water holes dry up in the dry season.

Transhumant husbandry is generally a periodic, seasonal movement of livestock to use seasonal pastures. The term derives from the Latin, humus (soil). It applies equally to the system of husbandry based on the intermittent movement of stock which may be necessary because of the seasonal scarcity of resources.

Transhumant husbandry concerns the management and exploitation of livestock during their greater or lesser movements from the base area. Once they have reached these grazings, the livestock can move to specific lands attached. This form of husbandry is characterised by strong specialisation in the village population between the shepherds and herders and the cultivators. In Europe, transhumance is practised between areas of low altitude, where animals are stabled during the winter, and areas of high alpine pastures. Transhumance of cattle has been known for a very long time in the Mediterranean basin. It is still found in areas of Spain, Italy, the Balkans and in Mediterranean France.

In sub-Saharan Africa, where the mobility of animals is an essential characteristic of husbandry and in many regions is a condition of their survival, transhumance remains very strong. Sedentary husbandry is found in areas of abundant natural resources all year round. This form of husbandry includes the management and use of livestock, where the movements take place within the same area of farmland. It is practised in association with or is complimentary to working the land. There can also be a system of agropastoralism surrounding the villages.
CHOUDHURY, K., AND JANSEN, L. J. M., 1999

7.A.7 **Aquaculture**

Aquaculture (F); Acuicultura (E)

According to the definition currently used by FAO for statistical purposes:

"Aquaculture is the farming of aquatic organisms including fish, molluscs, crustaceans and aquatic plants. Farming implies some sort of intervention in the rearing process to enhance production, such as regular stocking, feeding, protection from predators. Farming also implies individual or corporate ownership of the stock being cultivated." CHOUDHURY, K., and JANSEN, L. J. M., 1999

Aquaculture requires access to appropriate areas of land and water. In freshwater resources these are either privately owned or in some cases are nationalised. In marine areas these are commonly held by the state and users require an appropriate lease or other legal interest to allow them to use the required area. Increasingly, the environmental fragility of coastal zones is making it necessary for the proposed use to be considered in detail from land use planning and environmental impact perspectives.

7.A.8 **Arboriculture**

Arboriculture (F); Arboricultura (E)

Arboriculture is the intensive culture of trees in isolation, in a small group or in an orchard depending on the intention. FAO, 1978

Arboriculture includes small scale forestry for village wood requirements. It is based on the planting and supervision of fast growing tree species in groups or in rows on the boundaries of parcels.

IMAGE 9

7.A.7 Aquaculture

Model fish farm. Fish fry production: cast-netting in a shallow fish pond. Fish fry are produced for common carp, Chinese carp, tilapia and silver barb. Lack of mechanization and high cost of pond construction results in shallow seasonal ponds being typical of aquaculture in Laos. The project organizes training of farmer groups in improved production techniques that take into account the climatic and economic conditions of their provinces.

K. Pratt, FAO photo.

7.C.1 Common pasture / grazings
Vaine pâture (F)

Common pasture is exercised on specific land after the harvest for the animals of the inhabitants of the same village.

Common pasture is a recognised right either by title or by usage from time immemorial of the inhabitants of a village to send their stock to graze on the land of another's, except on enclosed properties or on sown grass, between the harvest and the drilling of a new crop.

The system of common pasture is very widespread in the rural African environment

7.C.2 Community forest
Forêt communautaire (F); Forestería comunitaria (E)

A community forest is "a tree-dominated ecosystem managed for multiple community values and benefits by the community".
DUINKER, P., 1994

Community forestry is based in the local control over, and enjoyment of the benefits from, the local forest resource. These benefits are not simply monetary, nor are they derived exclusively from timber production, but may vary with the many values associated with forest ecosystems, including cultural, spiritual, social, medicinal, ecological, recreational, aesthetic and economic values.
CURRAN, D., and M'GONIGLE, M., 1997

Community forestry initiatives:

- support the control, management and use of forest and tree resources by local communities
- respect social, economic and cultural relationships between people and forests
- involve decentralized and participatory approaches to forest management
- and assume that the best stewards of the world's forests are the populations living in and around them FAO, 1997

IMAGE 10

7.C.3 Crop rotation

Crop rotation in wetlands in Zimbabwe. Maize, rice and groundnuts are alternated and grown side by side with maize and groundnuts on raised ground. The water level is controlled by a sluice gate so the land is irrigated all year round. This has resulted in 8 tons per hectare yield instead of an average 2 tons per hectare before the project.

G. Diana, FAO photo.

7.C.3 **Crop rotation**

Assolement / Rotation des cultures (F);
Rotación de cultivos (E)

A crop rotation is a repetitive cultivation of an ordered succession of crops (or crops and fallow) on the same land. One cycle often takes several years to complete.
CHOUDHURY, K., and JANSEN, L. J. M., 1999

7.E.1 **Extensive / intensive**

Extensif / intensif (F); Extensivo / intensivo (E)

Extensive and intensive refer to the relative levels of use of the factors of land, labour and capital in production.

The terms extensive and intensive (or extensification or intensification when referring to the process) are relative concepts that have many meanings. In classical economics, they express the nature of the relationship between the factors of production: land, labour and capital. More specifically, they describe the relative importance of the factors of labour and capital in comparison with land.

Intensive production is production where the other factors of production, labour and capital, are used relatively abundantly compared with land. In this sense intensification is an increase of labour and or of capital used relative per unit of surface area. Production techniques are referred to as "labour intensive" or "capital intensive". This approach puts the accent on the quantities of inputs per unit of surface area.

7.F.1 **Fajenda**

Fazenda (F)

A fajenda is a great estate in Brazil and is most frequently used for extensive grazing. It is held as an investment and as an object of prestige, rather than purely for its productive capacity.
CHOUDHURY, K., AND JANSEN, L. J. M., 1999

7.F.2 **Fallow land**

Jachère / Mettre en jachère (F); Barbecho (E)

Fallow land is land set aside from farming to allow soil fertility to regenerate.

Fallow usually refers to land set aside for at least one season, and sometimes for periods of up to ten years or more. It may also refer to the period between the harvest of one crop and the planting of the next crop.

The practice tends to disappear with intensification of agricultural production.

7.F.3 **Farm tenancy**

Fermage (F); Arrenar fincas, garnjas o estancias (E)

A farm tenancy is a contractual agreement whereby the tenant farmer, the lessee, agrees a tenancy with the landowner, the lessor. The tenancy will identify the piece of land leased, together with the other terms and conditions, including rent.

In many countries farm tenancies have in the past been unwritten agreements. Partly as a result it has been common for the state to enact laws protecting some forms of tenancies and allowing certain assumptions as to the terms and conditions that can be statutorily assumed. FAO, 2001

7.F.4 **Farmer**

Agriculteur / Agricultrice (F); Agricultuor / Agricultora (E)

A farmer is "The principal decision-maker involved in the management of a farm who is usually but not always the head of the household. Sometimes the choice of principal decision-maker will be somewhat arbitrary since decision-making may sometimes be segregated for different farm activities." FAO, 1985

7.F.5 Farmholding / enterprise
Exploitation agricole (F)

A farm holding describes both an area of land, typically a working farm, and the possession of an area of farm land. The term does not include any implication of the legal rights by which the land is held, and it includes therefore both tenants and owners of land.

7.F6 Forest
Forêt (F); Bosque / Bosque comercial (E)

A forest is defined as:
"Land with tree crown cover (or equivalent stocking level) of more than 10% and area of more than 0.5ha. The trees should be able to reach a minimum height of 5m at maturity in situ. May consist either of closed forest formations where trees of various storeys and undergrowth cover a high proportion of the ground or of open forest formations with a continuous vegetation cover in which tree crown cover exceeds 10%. Young natural stands and all plantations established for forestry purposes which have yet to reach a crown density of 10% or tree height of 5m are included under forest, as are areas normally forming part of the forest area which are temporarily unstocked as a result of human intervention or natural causes but which are expected to revert to forest.
CHOUDHURY, K., and JANSEN, L. J. M., 1999

7.F.7 Forest area closed to grazing animals
Défense ou mise en défens (F)

Closed forest areas are put in place to protect young trees from grazing animals.

7.F.8 Forest class
Forêt classée (F)

Forest class is a specific class identified under a classification system. A forest classification system may deal with several different perspectives. Some relate to productivity and production with "age class" identifying the age of a stand of trees usually on a ten or twenty year band, and "forest land class" dealing with production potential. Protection related systems identify specific areas for varying degrees of protection. These latter may include specific measures of management and protection for the defined areas thus identifying their production potential.

7.F.9 Forest law

Droit forestier (F)

Forest law comprises the package of laws and regulations governing production and protection of forests, as well as those that regulate the powers of the administration in forests subject to the forest law.

7.F.10 Forest policy

Politique forestière (F); Política forestal (E)

Forest policy, whether conceived at international, national or local levels, defines the overall strategies for production, management and protection of forests. These policies are generally written into a planning document that is revised periodically. Ten years would be an appropriate time frame for this, given the long term characteristics of forestry.

These plans might include:

- development of the forestry resource
- need for forest products
- requirements for training and employment of forestry workers
- measures for protection, production, management and processing that will be necessary

7.G.1 Grazing contract / licence

Contrat de pâturage (F); Contrato de pastoreo (E)

A grazing contract or licence is a legal contract for an agreement, for example between a farmer and a grazier, specifying the terms under which the latter can use the identified land of the former for grazing purposes.

Instituting grazing contracts can take place in situations where there is a growing shortage of land and/or competition between agricultural and pastoral activities. These situations put an end to or throw into question the traditional equilibrium provided by customary use rights and monetarisation of exchange replaces customary mutual assistance.

7.H.1 Home grazing territory
Terroir d'attache (F)

The concept of home grazing territory (*terroir d'attache*) refers to a legally identified area in which pastoralists and agro-pastoralists reside for a large part of the year and to which they return following the period of transhumance.

The term *terroir d'attache* (home grazing territory) was developed under the Rural Code in Niger to deal with pastoral land holding systems.

These territories are organised to provide access to key resources including watering places and areas where certain types of crops or pastures are found. They may include areas where wild produce can be found.

Several groups have non-exclusive rights to these territories and may need to negotiate with each other access to these resources. LEONARD, R., and LONGBOTTOM, J., 2000

7.I.1 Intensification and land ownership

Intensification of production is related to land ownership in several ways.

Intensive agriculture or livestock husbandry use labour, capital and/or knowledge more intensively per unit of land area and achieve higher rates of production per hectare.

Intensification of agricultural production is related to pressure on the land or to lucrative field of activity. Scarcity of land leads to shortening of rotation periods, in other words the frequency of cultivation increases per unit of time or space.

Where production is limited to a relatively small area, it is compensated, if possible, by raised production per unit of surface area. This results from the introduction of:

> more productive varieties which respond better to inputs
> species of higher calorific value such as tubers in place of cereals
> higher value added cultivation; fruiticulture or market gardening

7.L.1 Latifundium

Latifundium (F); Latifundio (E)

A latifundium is a very large property characterised by:

> large size, running from several hundred hectares to tens of thousands of hectares
> very low productivity of the land which is often devoted to extensive grazing
> supplemented by subsistence crops provided by the people living on the land tied to the landlord on whom they are both personally and financially dependent.

These large estates are most numerous in Latin America where they are called haciendas, estancias or fajendas. Agrarian reforms resulted in their disappearance in Eastern Europe. They have been reduced and modernised in Southern Europe but are still found in the Middle East. BRUNET, R., et al, 1993

7.M.1 Manure contract

Contrat de confiage / Contrat de fumure (F)

A manure contract is an agreement where the herders supply the animals' manure to the farmers' land.

Traditionally in West Africa, farmers left the keeping of their stock to herders under a manure contract. The fields may benefit from the animals' dung in several ways:

- the farmer invites the herder to put the animals on his fields in the dry season, providing the possibility of watering the cattle and of manuring the fields
- the herder sells the manure to the farmer
- the stock are driven through the fields during the dry season – but in this case the quantities of fertilisers restored to the field are reduced

With the tensions that have tended to develop between farmers and herders, the practice of manure contracts has tended to disappear.

7.M.2 Mariculture

Mariculture is the farming of aquatic organisms including fish, molluscs, crustaceans and aquatic plants specifically in marine areas. As with aquaculture, farming in this context implies some sort of intervention in the rearing process to enhance production, such as regular stocking, feeding, protection from predators. Farming also implies individual or corporate ownership of the stock being cultivated."
CHOUDHURY, K., and JANSEN, L. J. M., 1999

Mariculture requires access to appropriate areas of coastal and marine land and water. In marine areas the marine areas are commonly held by the state and users require an appropriate lease or other legal interest to allow then to use the required area. Increasingly, the environmental fragility of coastal zones is making it necessary for the proposed use to be considered in detail from land use planning and environmental impact perspectives.

7.O.1 Orchard
Verger (F); Huerta / Vergel (E)

An orchard is an area planted with fruit trees. Orchards are often not defined in isolation from gardens.

IMAGE 11

7.M.2 Mariculture

Mariculture students in India cultivate mullet and prawns in the Institute of "wet lab" where physiology and nutrition experiments are conducted.

I. de Borhegyi, FAO photo.

IMAGE 12

7.O.1 Orchard

Orchard of Golden apples in Afghanistan.

M. Griffin, FAO photo.

7.P.1 **Park / enclosure**
Parc (F); Parque (E)

The park or enclosure is a typical part of sub-Saharan agrarian systems. The park or enclosure emerges during land/forest clearances as a regular and systematic population of trees that are retained, looked after, and improved because of their utility. GUKONU, E., 1991

7.P.2 **Pastoral land**
Espace pastoral (F)

Pastoral land is land used by pastoralists and shepherds for grazing livestock.

The term pastoral land refers to the use and management of resources which allow animal husbandry. It includes areas of natural vegetation such as savannah and forest as well as agricultural lands where the animals are put to the common grazing after the harvest. Equally important to this use are all of the necessary developments including the seasonal pastures (transhumance), the rights of way, the wells, the fixed and itinerant camping sites and others.

The Touareg Kel Dinnik in the Tahoua region of **Niger** occupy an area that does not belong to them, but over which they have more of a prior right of use.

Whoever digs a well has the water at their disposal and, although they have priority, they cannot prevent a stranger from drinking there. The stranger would not, without compensation, water his animals before him …

Although the stranger cannot be prevented from coming as well, the limit to this right is the danger for the first occupier caused by intrusion into his patoral land, and the damage caused to his stock…
CHOUDHURY, K., AND JANSEN, L. J. M., 1999

7.P.3 Pastoral land rights
Droits fonciers pastoraux (F)

Pastoral land rights are principally exercised over the resources of the home grazing territories based on the rules on the use of watering places. The pastoral communities exercise their effective but not exclusive management powers over land and water resources. They grant prior rights of access and reserve access rights for non-indigenous groups on the basis of consensus. The right to control watering places allows the communities to manage the use of the pastures as a function of the availability of water.

7.P.4 Pastoralist
Pasteur (F); Pastor / Vaquero (E)

A pastoralist looks after grazing livestock, as a shepherd, goatherd, swineherd, or cowherd in a way of life which is essentially livestock husbandry. A nomad is a pastoralist.

The term does not describe an activity, it is a way of life, and a form of society.

7.P.5 Pasture
Pâturage (F); Pastizal / Hacer pastar / Apacentar / Pastoreo (E)

Pasture is natural or artificial grassland where animals graze.

7.P.6 Pasture / grazing land rights
Pacage / pacager (F)

In the past, during the 16th Century, pasture rights (*pacage)* designated a right, a time and a place for grazing.

Natural grasslands with typically low productivity would not generally support pasture rights without care and maintenance and resolution of the difficulties such as those of access or of rocky outcrops.

IMAGE 13

7.P.6 Pasture / grazing land rights

Farmer with buffaloes grazing by a river at the edge of a rice field in Cambodia.

G. Bizarri, FAO photo

By extension, pasture rights also include the grazing of animals. The right of pasture on communal land near a village can involve the differentiation of herds and production in a mixed population of sedentary cultivators and herders.

*In the central delta of the **Niger**, the hariima is a communal grazing land of the village near to the village settlement and under the care of the village chief (or grazing chief) who keeps order and manages access. These pastures are exclusively reserved for one category of animals, milk cows. The right of pasture is forbidden not only to non-indigenous livestock herders, but also to the garci (transumant herds) of the village. These pasture lands and the droving rights of way cannot be cultivated.*
CHOUDHURY, K., AND JANSEN, L. J. M., 1999

7.P.7 Peasant

Paysan / Paysanne (F); Campesino / Campesina (E)

A peasant is a countryman, typically one who works on the land as a small farmer or labourer.

7.P.8 Peri-urban agriculture

Agriculture péri-urbaine (F); Agricultura periurbana (E)

Peri-urban agriculture refers to farm units close to town which operate intensive semi- or fully commercial farms to grow vegetables and other horticulture, raise chickens and other livestock, and produce milk and eggs. FAO, 2000

The FAO position paper *Urban and peri-urban agriculture* distinguishes peri-urban agriculture from urban agriculture which refers to small urban areas used for growing crops and raising small livestock or milk cows for own-consumption or sale in neighbourhood markets. These areas may include vacant plots, gardens, verges, balconies and containers.

7.P.9 Pluriactivity

Pluriactivity is a term commonly used across Europe that refers to the multiple sources of incomes, both agricultural and non-agricultural, increasingly generated by farmers and members of their households.

A proportion of farmers and members of farm households have always had occupations or income sources other than farming – pluriactivity – but discussion of this is complicated by the different definitions used. These include:

> *diversification* of the business into areas other than traditional farming
> the range of jobs or activities that farmers and their families they do
> *non-farming income* of farmers and their families, includes unearned income sources, such as pensions and investments, as well as those associated with activities

7.P.10 Private forest

Forêt privée (F)

Private forest where the detailed operations are controlled by the common rules for all forest land, including felling permits.

7.Q.1 Quota

A quota is a specific quantity allocated as a part of a policy mechanism to restrict free markets, for example in production (agriculture), in exploitation (fisheries), in harvesting or felling (timber) and in importing. Quotas are very commonly used to try to direct and protect the agricultural, fisheries and forestry industries.

7.R.1 Rangeland
Parcours (F)

Parcours (rangeland) has no specific English equivalent, but is where there is a reciprocal customary right of common grazings between two or more communities. It also applies to seasonal pastures that have been long used by itinerant herdsmen.

> *In the Maghreb, the customary or legal right of pasture in the forest and in mountains is the benefice of specific tribes.*

7.R.2 Right of way / Droving rights
Couloir de passage / Couloir de parcours (F);
Corredores de paso / Caminos / Trochas /
Pistas de transhumancia (E)

Rights of way or droving rights are routes for driving livestock that avoid damaging the crops through which they pass.

The rights of way are generally between 50 and 200 metres wide, and may be dozens of kilometres in length. These rights of way are also known as stock routes or transhumance corridors and are very important in enabling livestock to be moved without significant conflict to the transhumant areas. Increased pressure on land is causing farmers to plough up these rights of way, leading to increased damage and conflict between sedentary cultivators and pastoralists.
LEONARD, R., and LONGBOTTOM, J., 2000

7.S.1 Scrubland
Friche (F)

Scrubland is colonised by characteristic forms of scrub vegetation typically after the cessation of cultivation.

Scrubland is not confined as the French term, friche, is to scrub vegetation or to areas abandoned after having been cultivated, without any expectation of returning to productive use. This latter characteristic distinguishes it from fallow land. Scrubland is characterised by poor land often scattered with woody and pasture plants.

7.S.2 Set aside

Set aside is a feature of agriculture policies in some countries where production is controlled by setting land aside from agricultural production.

Under the European Union's set aside scheme in 2000, for example, farmers had to set aside 10% of their land as a condition for receiving crop subsidies.

7.S.3 Share cropping (Share tenancy)

Métayage (F); Aparcería / Mediería (E)

Share cropping is a system of agricultural production where a landowner allows a share cropper to use the land in return for a share of the crop produced on the land.

Share cropping covers a wide range of different situations and types of agreement. In the United States it is an important system of production and the individual states have specific legal frameworks.

Share cropping has reduced considerably from historical levels in Europe, although it remains of significance, for example, in England and Wales and is increasing elsewhere as a rational solution to the very heavy capital costs of large scale modern farming. In Europe the most common approach is now for direct farming by the owner or tenant farming through a tenancy. Share cropping is found extensively in other countries, particularly, for example, in Latin America.

In Africa, there are different views as to the causes of the increase in sharecropping arrangements in recent years. Some attribute it to customary arrangements being degraded by contact with the market economy, others to increasing numbers of population displacements, and others to the increasing shortage of land.
CHOUDHURY, K., AND JANSEN, L. J. M., 1999; LEONARD, R., and LONGBOTTOM, J., 2000

Two main types of share cropping agreement exist in Ghana. An abusa tenant clears and cultivates at his own expense a tract of virgin land allocated to him by a land holder. The tenant pays a third of the annual produce in return for his use of the land. The abunu share cropper either receives a farm to cultivate or the funds to establish a farm, in return for half the annual produce. The farm is operated by the tenant, but ultimately belongs to the original landholder/donor. A third example is the dibi-ma-dibi ("I eat, you eat") arrangement found in the cocoa and coffee growing region between Togo and Ghana. This originally allowed an immigrant to acquire a quasi-permanent right of occupation and possession in exchange for clearing and planting the plot with cocoa. The parcel could be passed on to his heirs as long as the plantation was farmed. LEONARD, R., and LONGBOTTOM, J., 2000

7.S.4 Silviculture

Sylviculture (F); Silvicultura (E)

Silviculture is the application of forest ecology to the production of renewable goods and services for human society. It is not forest management but consists of actions taken at the level of individual stands to renew and enhance the forest crop to meet stand management objectives for timber, wildlife, recreation, landscape design, preservation, and water yield.

7.S.5 State forest

Forêt dominiale (F); Bosque nacional (E)

State forest is forest in public ownership managed by the state forestry service.

In ***Cameroon****, for example, the permanent forest areas are divided into the state forests, both protected areas and production forests, and the community forests.*

7.S.6 State forest administration
Forêt soumise (F)

Foret soumise (state forest administration) has no specific English equivalent, but is where the forest of the decentralised communities is put under the state forestry administration for management.

7.T.1 Tenant farmer / Lessee
Tenancier (F); Tenedor (E)

A tenant farmer is someone who holds a farm as a farmer or a share cropper, and especially a small tenanted farm held from a large estate.

7.T.2 Transhumance / Seasonal grazing lands
Transhumance / Parcours saisonnier (F); Libre pastoreo (E)

Transhumance is the movement of livestock to use seasonal grazings and water supplies. Transhumance often involves long distance movements of livestock, in some cases over as much as hundreds of kilometres. Increasing strains are put on relations between transhumant and sedentary farmers with severe droughts, increased herd sizes resulting from improved animal health and increased agricultural areas.
CHOUDHURY, K., AND JANSEN, L. J. M., 1999

7.T.3 Tree rights
Arbre (foncier de l') (F)

Tree rights are specific rights held in relation to trees and their products. Trees have many uses and rights associated with them. In Africa the long term nature of trees and their production has resulted in specific tenure of tree assets. There are four categories of rights:

> right to plant
> right to use
> right to disposal
> right to own or to inherit

CHOUDHURY, K., AND JANSEN, L. J. M., 1999

These rights may develop into rights over the land on which the tree is planted. As a result landholders in Africa are very reluctant to allow people with subsidiary interests, such as tenants, borrowers, share croppers and others, to plant trees for fear that they will acquire long term rights over the land. LEONARD, R., and LONGBOTTOM, J., 2000

The general approach to tree rights is that naturally generated trees are community property whereas planted trees are owned by the planter, although there are exceptions where ownership is determined by the underlying land ownership even though the trees are naturally generated. Gender restrictions on land ownership may also carry through to tree ownership, with societies where women are resricted from owning land often restricting or prohibiting tree planting and ownership by women. LEONARD, R., and LONGBOTTOM, J., 2000

7.U.1 Urban forest
Forêt urbaine (F)

Urban and peri-urban forestry are specific to urban and peri-urban areas. They are multi-functional with critical environmental functions, in addition to some food and non-food production functions. FAO, 2000

7.W.1 Wood clearing
Essart / Essartage (F)

A wood clearing is land which is made cultivable after the clearance of the timber.

REFERENCES CHAPTER 7

CHOUDHURY, K., and JANSEN, L. J. M., Eds.,*Terminology for Integrated Resources Management and Planning*, FAO/UNEP, Rome, 1999

CURRAN, D., and M'GONIGLE, M., *First Nations Forests: Community Management as Opportunity and Imperative*, Discussion Paper D97-7, University of Victoria, Canada, 1997

DUINKER, P., *Community Forests in Canada*, The Forestry Chronicle, Vol. 70, No.6, November/December. 1994

FAO, *Le rôle des forêts dans le développement des collectivités locales*, FAO, Rome, 1978

FAO, *Farm Management Glossary*, FAO Agricultural Services Bulletin 63, FAO Rome, 1985

FAO, *People and Forests - Community Forestry at FAO*, FAO, Rome, Italy, 1997

FAO, *Urban and peri-urban agriculture*, position paper accessed at http://www.fao.org/unfao/bodies/COAG/COAG15/X0076e.htm, FAO, Rome, 2000

FAO, *Good Practice Guidelines for Agricultural Leasing Arrangements.* FAO Land Tenure Studies No. 2. Rome. 2001

GUKONU, E., *L'arboriculture*, in LE BRIS, E., LE ROY, E, and MATHIEU, *L'appropriation de la terre en Afrique noire*, Karthala, Paris, 1991

LEONARD, R., and LONGBOTTOM, J., *Land Tenure Lexicon: A glossary of terms from English and French speaking West Africa,* International Institute for Environment and Development (IIED), London, 2000

GENERAL BIBLIOGRAPHY

General bibliography

ACCT, *Dictionnaire d'agriculture,* Paris, 1997

BRUCE, J.W., and MIGOT-ADHOLLA, S.Eds., *Searching for Land Tenure Security in Africa*, Kendall/Hunt Publishing Co, Iowa, 1994

BRUNET R., FERRAS, R., and THERY, H., *Les mots de la géographie. Dictionnaire critique*, Montpellier, Maison de la Géographie, 1993

CHOUDHURY, K., and JANSEN, L. J. M., Eds.,*Terminology for Integrated Resources Management and Planning*, FAO/UNEP, Rome, 1999

CIPARISSE, G., Ed., *Thésaurus multilingue du foncier. Version française,* FAO, Rome, 1999

CLEMENT, J. M., Ed., *Larousse Agricole*, Paris, 1981

CORNU, G., Ed. *Vocabulaire juridique,* PUF, Paris, 1990

CUBRILO, M., and GOISLARD, C., *Bibliographie et lexique du foncier en Afrique noire,* Paris, 1998

de BONNEVAL, L., *Systèmes agraires, systèmes de production. Vocabulaire français-anglais avec index anglais*, Paris, 1993

GEORGE, P., *Dictionnaire de la géographie.* Paris, 1990

LEBEAU, R., *Les grands types de structures agraires dans le monde.* Paris, 1996

LE BRIS, E., LE ROY, E., LEIMDORFER, F., *Enjeux fonciers en Afrique noire*, Paris, Karthala, 1983

LE BRIS, E., LE ROY, E., and MATHIEU, P., *L'appropriation de la terre en Afrique noire*, Karthala, Paris, 1991

LEONARD, R., and LONGBOTTOM, J., *Land Tenure Lexicon: A glossary of terms from English and French speaking West Africa,* International Institute for Environment and Development (IIED), London, 2000

MAZOYER, M., and ROUDART, L., *Histoire des agricultures du monde. Du néolithique à la crise contemporaine,* Paris, 1997

PARENT, S., *Dictionnaire des sciences de l'environment,* Paris, 1991

PLATTEAU, J.-Ph., *Land Reform and Structural Adjustment in Sub-Saharan Africa: Controversies and Guidelines,* FAO, Rome, 1993

RUTHENBERG, H., *Farming Systems in the Tropics,* Oxford, 1976

WORLD COMMISSION ON ENVIRONMENT AND DEVELOPMENT, *Our Common Future*, Oxford University Press, Oxford, 1987

WUNDERLICH, G., Ed., *Agricultural landownership in transitional economies*, University Press of America, Maryland, 1995

*** *Un droit inviolable et sacré, la propriété,* ADEF, Paris, 1991

*** *Mémento de l'agronome,* Paris, 1993

GENERAL INDEX OF TERMS

GENERAL INDEX OF TERMS